The analysis of
Handwriting
Personality and Character

is b

...to David

Acknowledgements
Immense gratitude to two gifted and hardworking calligraphers:
Meic Morgan-Finch and Peter Halliday.

Plus grateful thanks and acknowledgements to: (*France*) Lycée Français Charles de Gaulle, (*Germany*) Consulate General of the Federal Republic of Germany and the Goethe Institute, (*Holland*) Gaby Meerwyk and Cindy Hofland, (*Italy*) Education Department — Italian Consulate General, (*Spain*) Senor Garcia (Cheshire) and the Spanish Embassy, (*United Kingdom*) The Archives — Chester Castle, Miss Barbara Cartland, Jan Cookson of the Museum of the History of Education — Leeds University, Emma Donnelly Simpson, David Gattie (Prontaprint), Christine Horton, Barbara Jones, Bernard Manning, Peter Morrison MP, Frank Muir, National Postal Museum, Carl Pierce, Nicholas Pierce, Timothy Pierce, Arthur Scargill, Robert (Bob) Symes, Barry Took, Frankie Vaughan, Victoria and Albert Museum, Victoria First School — Chester, The Duke of Westminster, Jim and Sylvia Ward, (*USA*) Gloria Lalumia, (*USSR*) Soviet Embassy.

The analysis of Handwriting

Personality and Character

Diane Simpson

A & C Black · London

First published 1985 by A & C Black (Publishers) Ltd
35 Bedford Row, London WC1R 4JH

Copyright © Diane Simpson 1985

Simpson, Diane
   The analysis of handwriting.
   1. Graphology
   I. Title
   155.28ı2   BF891
   ISBN 0-7136-5509-7

Design by Krystyna Hewitt

Typeset in 12/13pt Goudy Old Style by Armitage TypoGraphics Ltd, Huddersfield

Printed and bound in Great Britain by R J Acford, Chichester

Contents

Beginnings

Generally speaking, handwriting analysis can be described both as a science and as an art; my preference is to define the subject as a scientific art. Critics, in an effort to diminish the subject, often comment that handwriting analysis cannot be taken seriously because it is not an exact science. This is nonsense and is negated by the fact that psychology, meteorology and certain medical practices are not exact sciences any more than many other entirely reputable and acknowledged branches of scientific study.

The dictionary definition of the word 'art' includes such descriptions as 'skill, especially human skill as opposed to nature; skilful execution as an object in itself; thing in which skill may be exercised, especially certain branches of learning which serve as intellectual instruments for more advanced studies', and so on. Handwriting is most definitely a human skill, the skilful execution of which is very much the object of the exercise. Handwriting is certainly an intellectual instrument to be used as an aid to more advanced studies.

Handwriting analysis, then, is a *scientific art*. It is not an end in itself, but it can provide a most useful tool in the overall assessment of human personality. Handwriting analysis, otherwise known as graphology, has its roots buried in the mists of time; but it is only during the last hundred years and the advent of mass literacy that extensive research has been able to be undertaken.

Erroneously linked with palmistry and astrology, handwriting analysis has not been taken as seriously as it undoubtedly should be. It is, however, used as a tool of measurement by an ever increasing group of enlightened recruitment consultants and psychology-based analysts throughout the world. Their findings prove over and over again that handwriting analysis is one of the most accurate and fascinating methods of assessing personality traits known to mankind. There are other methods of assessment which, although equally accurate, contain responses which can be learned and implanted artificially. Any such manoeuvre is easily detected when attempted within a sample of writing and therefore attempts to deceive the analyst are doomed to fail.

There is no 'magic' formula attached to the analysis of writing...it consists solely of the careful application of measurement plus an equal portion of commonsense and knowledge. *Shortcuts always detract from accuracy* and should be avoided rather than sought after.

A brief history

In order to begin to understand the process of analysis we must first consider our raw material...writing. Writing takes the form of a series of functional and three-dimensional objects. Each letter, each word, each sentence is an object which has height, breadth and depth. Before your eyes at this moment are a series of shapes which comprise an alphabet. An alphabet is a series of symbols representing the sounds of speech. Writing exists to be read and, therefore, legibility is an essential virtue if the communication of the writer's thoughts is to be successfully achieved.

At first a mere aid to memory, writing took the form of a series of marks or notches which illustrated and recorded the writer's ideas. As messages became more complicated notches were replaced by pictures, and the number of pictures in any one message lengthened to avoid ambiguity. After all, it is one thing to record the number of eggs laid in a single season and quite another to record successfully the intimate details of a tribal squabble. Pictorial images were of necessity replaced by symbols. Communication demands were (and still are!) an everchanging and developing hunger; therefore, in order to progress, writing symbols were adapted and refined according to need. The fact that the evolution of communication symbols continues is borne out by a few moments' contemplation of some of the latest machine languages...

Although it is known that more than 200,000 years lie between cave paintings and present-day writing, just how the step from pictures to symbols was made and by whom is something about which we can only surmise. However, we do know that the development of alphabets which appear today has taken many thousands of years and may be attributed to relatively few people. The spread of the written word must be largely attributed to the missionary zeal of a variety of religious leaders whose desire to spread their word was not to be inhibited by the fact that they could not do it in person; their machinations were entrusted to solid rock, clay tablets, papyrus scrolls, illuminated manuscripts, and the like.

Up until the early fifteenth century and the birth of the printing press, reading and writing were relevant only to the ruling classes. The correlation between different writing styles was greatly inhibited by the personal foibles of the writers. With the advent of printing and the ensuing mass-produced literature, the need for legibility and hence a measure of uniformity made itself apparent.

Until the twelfth century book production had two main markets: elaborate publications for the royal courts, and religious publications. The scholarship of the Arabs, Greeks and Jews led to a need for, and subsequently the creation of, independent centres of learning which called for a wider range of books about mathematics, astronomy, music and philosophy. Translations were undertaken and writers began to write in their own languages instead of confining themselves to the classics. As a result, more people began to read and commission books. Papermakers, illuminators, book binders and scribes were in great demand. However, unless a member of the public had connections with the Church or a wealthy household, the opportunity to handle a book, let alone read one, was somewhat remote.

The profession of 'stationer' came into being along with the ever increasing demand for books. The would-be customer consulted the 'stationer' as to price, subject and quality of the required work. The stationer, acting as middle man between customer and craftsman, would co-ordinate the commissioning of the book. Stationers would also commission books for sale 'off the peg' in their own premises.

Newly formed universities and schools began to call for more books as well. Scribes had to meet immense demands, but even as thousands of them were each striving to produce a few pages of writing in a day the first German printing presses began to churn out hundreds of pages an *hour*.

In the early stages of printing, space was left for the illuminator to embellish the page. But the days of the scribes were, to say the least, numbered. As more books became available, more people learned to read and, in turn, individuals then wanted to be able to write: thus, the writing masters took the stage. Inumerable writing manuals became available, each in its author's own inimitable style. Fashions in writing styles appeared, only to become 'old fashioned' in due course and to be replaced by the next in line. Throughout Europe handwriting styles began to develop and were refined according to the dictates of necessity. The more ornate, formal hands were reserved for legal documentation while faster, simplified writing was better for personal usage.

Unless the writing masters possessed immense artistic skill and, as a result, could make an artistic living, they had little choice but to supplement their writing skills by passing on their knowledge in teaching reading, writing and arithmetic — the birth of the school teacher no less!

The stationer still exists and, on occasion, is still a middle man, but no longer between the scribe and the book buyer — largely between the customer and the manufacturers of writing paper and greeting cards.

Writing styles

It is not possible to chronicle exactly the order in which writing styles came into popular use, as they tended to overlap and also to appear in a variety of forms. The following pages contain examples of writing trends which will serve as signposts to the norm of the day. For example, greatly elaborate writing in the 1980s, unless an art form, may be deemed to be the result of a certain affectation on behalf of the writer and certainly not a reflection of the way the writer in question was originally taught to write. Whereas seemingly extravagantly embellished writing from the eighteenth century could very well be the exact form learned in school.

When analysing any sample of writing it is advisable to check the likely 'Copybook' script. This is especially the case where the writing under scrutiny is from a different country or age from that of the analyst.

As many samples and as much writing as possible must be examined for the purposes of analysis. It is not possible to assess personality from a few words, any more than it is possible from a few actions! Originals, although sometimes unobtainable, are by far preferable to copies which leave pressure to be only guessed at.

Content may be fictitious and must be largely ignored so that any written 'red herrings' are not allowed to blur the truth. A combination of discipline and practice will enable the analyst to resist absorbing content until at least half of the analysis has been completed.

Necessary tools are a transparent ruler, a transparent protractor, an *empty* ballpoint pen, tracing paper, and a pencil. A magnifying glass is a useful but optional extra.

A full analysis will *always* take hours to complete. If you can do it in less time, then you are not doing it properly!

A collection of Copybook styles

Once having mastered the rudiments of handwriting analysis many people, wishing to exercise and test their newly acquired ability, turn to writing such as that of historical figures, media idols or foreign penfriends in order to know personalities directly (instead of through the prejudices of historians, the imagination of public relation officials or disguise created by distorted writing content). However, one has only to compare present day British writing with that of fifty years ago or with today's American writing to realise the immense difference teaching methods can and do make to the appearance of writing. Therefore, a knowledge of the way a writer was actually taught to write provides an invaluable aid to accurate analysis. To this end I have designed the following chapter as a safety net for people who wish to analyse writing which was learned in a time or at a location different from their own. A simple check on the idiosyncrasies of the writing style learned by the writer will ensure that any deviations from the analyst's writing norm will not be erroneously classified as emanating from within the writer's personality.

The following collection of writing styles illustrates the major changes that have occurred in writing styles and, deliberately, is not totally comprehensive. Fads rose and fell within the writing world with the speed and regularity of the proverbial fiddler's elbow. To chart them all would be an extremely time-consuming task that would achieve little for graphology and would be practically impossible to complete. My collection can certainly be added to by the avid collector, but in itself provides a most adequate tool for any graphologist.

1400s — present day

I really must give pride of place to *italic*...if for no other reason than for sheer endurance under the strain of so many copyings! In the 1400s italic began to be used for the writing of papal briefs. It was soon used in royal circles and was widely adopted. The first book to teach italic was published in Rome in 1522 by the writing master Arrighi.

Italic in all its many versions has appeared and reappeared through the centuries, sometimes learned as a schoolroom norm and sometimes as a self-taught attempt to improve writing style. Beloved of calligraphers throughout the ages, italic is still taught, albeit at the calligrapher's elbow rather than in the schoolroom.

It should not be forgotten that the Copybook models were usually engraved, so writers' attempts with a goose quill made rather scrappy copies.

abcdefghijklmnopqrstuvwxyz

ABCDEFGHIJKLMNOPQR STUVWXYZ 1234567890

1500s

The writing masters held sway. The educated classes wrote, the masses did not.

abcdefghiklmnoppqqrsstuxyz

Q st st ffffß

Arrighi – Italian, 1520.

A abcdeefggbiklmnopqrsstuxyz

AABB[CDDEEFFGGHHJIkLLMMNNOPQQRR

sSSTTUVVXYZ

Ludovico Vicentino – Italian, 1523.

Francisco Lucas – Spanish, 1577.

Andreas Brun – Spanish, 1500s.

abcdefghijklmnopqrstuvwxyz

ABCDEFGHIJKLMNOPQ

RSTUVWXYZ

Gothic – German, 1500s. (There were subsequent revivals of Gothic lettering and it is still turned to when a quaint or medieval 'look' is required.)

1600s

Martin Billingsley – British, 1618.

Richard Gething – British, 1642.

William Elder – British, 1691.

1700s

Joseph Champion – British, 1760s.

George Shelley – British, 1709.

George Bickham – British, 1743. (This style is known as Copperplate or English round-hand.)

Thomas Weston – British, 1726.

1800s

Schreibschrift (the name of the script, not the inventor!) – German.

Thomas E. Hill – USA, 1870s.

Vere Foster – British, 1898. This style heralded the introduction of the 'Civil Service' hand.

It should be noted that a cheap metal nib became available for the first time in 1830; hitherto the quill was the more commonplace writing implement.

In the mid eighteen hundreds 'The Ladies' Hand' was introduced, presumably because it was thought that the female, being a weak and genteel creature, was unable to meet the demands of the ordinary writing of the day. The Ladies' Hand was small, rather spiky and contained no difference between thick and thins. The upperarm was not employed in the writing movement, which resulted in a rather 'prissy' hand. Extremely small writing came into vogue and also Cross Writing (filling the page horizontally and then beginning all over again by turning the page a quarter turn and writing across the already written lines creating a 'lattice' pattern). Fortunately the Victorian 'Ladies' Hand' passed away along with frilled table legs, and only remains in our memories in the form of the oft held and *erroneous* conviction that the sex of writers can be determined by their writing.

1900s

Today's trends are towards simplicity, although glimpses of the past can still be traced in some of the current scripts.

ABCDEFGHIJKLMNOPQRSTU
VWXYZ

abcdefghijklmnopqrstuvwxyz

Marion Richardson — British. Introduced in 1935, this style was intended to simplify the writing process and started a trend which resulted in:

ABCDEFGHIJKLMNOPQR
STUVWXYZ

abcdefghijklmnopqrstuvwxyz

Print-script — British, 1980s.

Dutch, 1980s.

German, 1980s.

Palmer Script – USA, 1980s.

French, 1980s. This is sometimes taught with a slight slant to the right.

Spanish, pre-1970.

A B C D E F G H I J K L M N O P Q R J Z U V

W X Y Z ¿? ¡!

a b c d e f g h i j k l m n o p q r s t u v x y z

Spanish, 1980s. Take note of the inverted question and exclamation marks which are placed *before* the sentence.

Italian, 1980s.

Russian, 1980s. This is a somewhat different alphabet, comprising 34 letters, but it is the way that Russian children are taught to write. The rules of analysis can be applied in the usual way.

Form level

The form level of writing is the means by which the analyst deduces whether a specific writing feature should be regarded in a negative or a positive light.

For instance, very light pressure, if regarded negatively, could mean that the writer was lethargic, neurotic or just plain feeble. A positive interpretation could point to the writer's sensitivity and refinement. Most writing features have negative and positive interpretations; therefore, understanding and being able to measure form level is of vital importance to every writing analyst.

To determine form level, a number of factors must be considered together: these are easy legibility, maintained speed, pleasingly aesthetic qualities and regular rhythm. It is the presence, or lack of it, of these four which makes writing, and therefore form level, 'good' or 'bad'.

To clarify further the importance of form level take a moment or two to consider another form of communication, i.e. speech. We can all recognise a good (or bad) speaking voice. A 'good' speaking voice (one with a high form level) flows into our ears — pleasantly modulated, punctuated by deliberate pauses rather than with hesitation or breathlessness, warm, interesting and always audible. When such a speaker begins to whisper, listeners become bright eyed in anticipation of the secrets they are about to hear.

A 'bad' speaker beginning to whisper does not cause the same response in his listeners. A 'bad' speaking voice (low form level) is poorly modulated and is punctuated by hesitation and perhaps breathlessness. Boring and frequently inaudible, such a voice irritates and often embarrasses listeners. This speaker's decision to whisper would interpret in a number of ways — all of them bad! Perhaps the speaker had become so overcome by nervousness that his voice had seized up or perhaps he was so wrapped up in saying his piece that maintaining voice level had not occurred to him; on the other hand, perhaps his poor speaking voice was due to his feeling unwell and the lapse into a whisper was just a minute away from a faint or worse.

Writing is body language frozen in ink. Writing is the spoken word enshrined in the memory of the writing surface. If you think of writing in terms of body language, the 'ideal' is that which reflects a healthy and self-assured individual, one whose movements are strong without expressing undue aggression, and gentle but not feeble. High form level writing glides purposefully over the page; it is aesthetically pleasing to look at, has individualistic formations and (most important of all) is clearly legible. A couple of good examples follow:

Dear Diane Simpson,

(Frank Muir)

Dear Diane,

(Barry Took)

Height, width, spacing and depth all contribute in their different ways, along with speed, angle and originality to reveal the variety, the balance and the sheer richness of personality.

Writing which may be carefully executed but slow and rigidly formed has a lower form level than fast flowing, spontaneous script that almost dances over the page. Think of the difference between the rigid correctness of the soldier on parade and the seemingly effortless flight of the smallest, most insignificant bird as it glides on the breeze.

A slow, rigid formation suggests anxiety to retain an image and perhaps a certain fear of losing control. Equally, many so-called 'beautiful' writings are the affectedly over-ornamented products of those people who wish to appear artistic or unusual and who are prepared to spend time on creating an 'image'. The form level of such writing is decidedly low.

Dear Miss Simpson

(Anon)

No. Man is a failure who has friends!

(Bernard Manning)

It will take time and experience to assess form level accurately. Each and every analyst must never forget to take his own personal taste and aesthetic judgement into consideration when evaluating the quality (or lack of it) of form level.

Size of writing

Copybook sizes may differ, but if a general rule of thumb is applied for purposes of convenience any disparity between interpretation and the rest of the analysis can be duly adjusted. For our purposes the norm will be a middle zone of 3mm (⅛″). Occasional small rises and falls are entirely normal; it is consistency in enlargement or diminishment that the analyst is seeking.

Small

There is a need to write slightly larger when using a thick pen to ensure legibility. Like a whisper, small writing does not set out to draw attention to itself. People with writing like this often confine themselves to relatively few friendships. Often rather inward looking and modest about their achievements, their motivation comes from within themselves.

If the writing is legible, small writing is often a sign of applied intelligence. These writers may have very high executive ability. Their judgement tends to be sound and their academic achievements high.

Small but illegible writing may be interpreted as a distinct sign of independence. These writers want other people to consider them to be something of an enigma and to have to work at understanding them. These are often quite 'difficult' types!

Medium

Whatever else they may do, these writers are usually prepared to conform to convention.

Large

Large writing commands attention. Occasional bursts of large writing are produced by us all, usually when we need to ensure that our writing is noticed and can be read easily.

Consistently large writing is indicative of the writer who constantly wants attention. Such writers often have a deep longing to achieve recognition and admiration. To be thought of as being a Great person (Nobel Prize and all!) would be the pinnacle of ambition. Negatively, these writers can be somewhat obtrusive with all their enthusiasm and what amounts to boastfulness. Positively, they may have 'larger than life' personalities and provide most entertaining companionship.

Mixed sizes

Although slight rises and falls within the size of the middle zone are entirely normal, extreme rises and falls must be examined with interest. Such changes in size denote marked mood swings, often of a childish nature. As a result, the writer's responses to overtures are likely to be inconsistent, perhaps tending towards the immature. Depending upon other facets of the writer's personality, this childishness may have a certain charm or, alternatively, it may be considered intensely irritating.

No change in size

Assuming that the writing is not typewriting, such uniformity of middle zone size may be interpreted as indicating self-discipline, lack of spontaneity, rigidity of approach and excessive adherence to conformity.

Speed of writing

Sheer practice does wonders for most things, including speed of writing, but practice alone will no more turn a frog into a prince than it will transform a dullard into a genius. As far as the speed of writing (or anything else) is concerned, we all develop our own personal velocity. This may vary according to the mood of the moment but generally speaking our individual paces are fixed. The careful, slow thinker will communicate carefully and slowly. The spontaneous, quick thinker will by virtue of his natural tendencies communicate (as he does everything else) in a spontaneous and quick way.

Although most people can rise to an occasion and have little choice but to quail beneath undue pressure, they usually prefer to trundle along at their own most comfortable physical and mental speeds. An individual writer's personal pace provides a clear signpost to his mental and physical agility.

When assessing the speed of writing try tracing it (a copy not the original!) with an empty ball point pen. It is possible to learn a great deal about both the writing and the writer in this way. Curved lines are easier to write than straight lines. A complete line is easier to write than a broken line. Large writing is easier to form than small writing. Dots slow writing down so at speed they turn into dashes. Speed tends to slant lots of things towards the 'goal' direction — think of a runner. Very speedy writing almost invariably has a right slant.

Pressure will lapse into a natural rhythm, combining both firm and light strokes. Writing which has just one pressure is not as fast as it might be.

Carry your empty ball point pen around with you and when you encounter interesting writing test it for speed. With high form standard writing you will discover that the writer has incorporated original and often fascinating ways of enhancing speed. Low form standard writing has an interest value all of its own; your pen will soon winkle out the time-consuming little foibles and missed opportunities which are scattered throughout such writing.

Three examples

Test the theory on the following three writing samples. Each is reproduced original size. Start slowly and then as you get used to the writer's personal rhythm you will be able to speed up. You will find that the sensation is strongly akin to the science fiction theory of mind transference. Allow your imagination some freedom . . . and you will discover that your mind has become a passenger inside someone else's head. It is their writing you have in front of you; having gained a somewhat clumsy control over the new body's fingers, begin to trace the writing. As you start to follow the lines which the 'other' brain made you will learn a great deal about the real owner of the body you temporarily inhabit...

One of the three samples was written by a politician, one by a prolific authoress and one by a showbusiness personality...Try their minds and bodies on for size. See if you can deduce which is which before turning to page 39 to learn their identities.

Assessment of speed

To analyse writing correctly it is of prime importance to assess speed. To aid assessment make a comparison with the speed of the spoken word. Very slow, disjointed, unrhythmical speech sounds strange and unnatural, and in the same way slow, disjointed, unrhythmical writing looks unnatural. However, it is important to look carefully at the likely Copybook style of the writer before making too many pronouncements. A simple comparison between the British 'Marion Richardson' style and the American 'Palmer' script reveals vast differences in letter formation even though since 1935 both styles have been taught, albeit in different countries. It is, therefore, little wonder that stepping back in time as well as over national boundaries can make the perfectly 'normal' Copybook writing of the day look distinctly strange.

ABCDEFGHI

Marion Richardson

ABCDEFGHI

Palmer

To speed the process of writing, simplifications have to be made. As the whole object of the enterprise is communication, simplifications that obstruct legibility must be interpreted negatively. Alternatively, the writer who is prepared to devote extra time to the insertion of additional ornamentation into his writing and who only succeeds in confusing the would-be reader is, to put it mildly, defeating the object of his exercise which is, presumably, to enhance the writing.

The verbal comparison is the speaker who, in an effort to speed up, resorts to a gabble, and his counterpart who attempts to improve his speech with the insertion of time-consuming, irritating and confusing affectations — *iacta alea est* (translation 'the die is cast' — if you see what I mean!)

Naturally speeded up writing flows smoothly. Simplifications do not detract from legibility but both save time and streamline the writing.

Writing may be written slowly so that it can be more easily read. View slowly written writing as you would slowly spoken words: if directed towards a child, a dimwit or a foreigner, fine, but if for the benefit of a normally functioning adult it would be tantamount to an insult.

'I HAVE TO GO SLOWLY SO THAT YOU CAN FOLLOW'

Slow writing implies calculation and/or self-consciousness.

Do not make the assumption that the writer who rarely writes will of necessity write slowly. Even near illiterates will find ways to speed up their scribings, usually by making them as short as possible or by missing out sections. Even the slowest brain moves faster than the most agile hand. The action of writing forces the writer to slow his thought processes down. Most of us find this at least mildly irritating and, as a result, the more we write the stronger we experience the urge to speed up. The first and the last pages of a long letter make an interesting barometer to measure the writer's self-discipline as he endeavours to maintain the initial level of legibility. If the writer is impatient the speeding-up process will become apparent on the first page, almost as soon as the pen is used.

Writing that begins quickly and then, as the lines of writing speed down the page, slows down is indicative of a writer who has taken stock of the situation and realised that he must gain control. Even the ultra-fast writer will usually slow down as he puts his signature to a letter.

You must investigate the ebbs and flows of writing speed with utmost care. If you encounter a puzzling feature, contemplate its verbal parallel, remembering as you do that both writing and speech are first and foremost methods of communication. Changes of speed in either medium must be regarded as plus factors if they enhance understanding and minus factors if they detract from understanding.

The first sample of writing on page 37 is from Peter Morrison M.P., the second is from Barbara Cartland, and the third is from Frankie Vaughan.

Zones

upper

middle

lower

All writing is divided into three distinct zones: upper, middle and lower. If you will allow your imagination to meander a little, I suggest that you equate these three zones with the three strata of population on a large ship.

future

present

past

The upper zone takes you onto the bridge. It is here that distant horizons are scanned and future voyages are envisaged. In personality terms the upper zone takes you up into the heady atmosphere of ambition, intellect, imagination, spiritual leanings and fantasy. In terms of time, this zone symbolises the future. Physically, this zone represents the head and shoulders.

The middle zone takes you onto the promenade deck to join the passengers whose preoccupation is with the company they keep. In personality terms the middle zone surrounds us with social life, everyday living, emotional expression and action. In terms of time, it is the present. Physically, this zone represents the torso.

The lower zone takes you down below decks. Here the engines are pounding along while the galley hums with activity and the maintenance men are ever watchful. In personality terms this zone represents unconscious drives necessary for survival. Biological appetites are here, as are material requirements and memory. In terms of time, this zone is the past. Physically, this zone represents the lower body.

The balance between the three zones is an excellent pointer to a writer's inner equilibrium. It is usual to find that one or other of the zones has achieved dominance over the other two zones. Alternatively one or other of the zones may have been suppressed in favour of the other zones or zone. Occasional fluctuations may be ignored, but consistent dominance or diminishment of a zone must be carefully examined.

When all three zones are consistently well-balanced and yet flexible in formation, the writer is exhibiting consistency within himself. Such writers are at ease with themselves and are capable of encountering and dealing with most situations with aplomb.

It is important to realise that dominance is not merely a matter of size: it can also be achieved by increased pressure or exaggerated elaboration. In the same way a zone may appear suppressed, not only by virtue of its diminished size but also by lack of pressure or elaboration.

Dominant upper zone

These writers have intelligence and ambition but may well lack the common sense, practicality or powers of organisation which are necessary to achieve their goals. The phrase 'head in the clouds' fits admirably. Their goals are often very far reaching. If the dominance is truly excessive, to the extent of appearing distorted, then fantasy may well be the major influence upon motivation — the 'Walter Mitty' syndrome!

Diminished upper zone

These writers lack imagination and do not place much emphasis on intellectual pursuits. Their motivation stems from more practical considerations. When the form level is high, these writers are often sociable, self-reliant types. When the form standard is low, materialism and the fulfilment of personal appetites take priority.

Dominant middle zone

These writers are most interested in the way they feel and what is taking place in their immediate circle. Writing with a dominant middle zone is often described as childish writing and, indeed, a reluctance to focus on anything that does not directly impinge upon personal circumstances is akin to a child's certainty that her or his place is situated close to the centre of the universe.

One of the results of this intense self-involvement is that these writers tend to award great importance to the most trivial events just because the events in question happen to touch their periphery...one could be forgiven for thinking that nobody had ever had dandruff before...

Such writers are often strong-willed and self-reliant but may lack the capacity to put 'self' to one side to attain goals. They need to be in the frontline and rarely, if ever, would function as some sort of understudy. Their personalities serve well as trade tools and they are often successful leaders. Whatever they involve themselves in, somehow they will gravitate to the front (although not necessarily to the top!)

Diminished middle zone

These writers are rarely to be found extolling their own virtues. If the form standard is high, a very small middle zone is often an indication that the writer is able to put his own immediate personal needs and desires to one side to achieve better and more far-reaching goals. Such writers may be quite creative but are unlikely to have much desire to enter the spotlight, their preference being for doing rather than being. Often very independent in their thinking, these writers are frequently found to have well sharpened powers of judgement and have many heads of state, leaders of industry and commerce, and great philosophers among their ranks.

Dominant lower zone

These writers are dominated by their instinctual drives. These are the *survivors* in every sense of the word. They are usually able to utilise a combination of down-to-earth organisation and instinctive 'gut' feelings to achieve their goals.

Such writers often have a great deal of stamina but it will be necessary for the analyst to investigate other aspects of handwriting to determine whether an individual is succumbing excessively to the influence of one particular drive and, as a result, not coping as well as he might do overall.

Diminished lower zone

A lower zone that is dwarfed by the other two zones is unusual. If you think back to the ship analogy, a stunted lower zone would represent a ship without a proper engine. How the ship had gone as far as it already had would be open to conjecture. There are a number of possibilities here. For instance, the ship (or the writer) might have been proceeding quite nicely until, for whatever reason, the 'engine' suddenly ceased to function. In handwriting terms the analyst might suspect a sudden trauma or immense fear. If, however, the diminished lower zone is a consistent feature of writing, the ship (writer) must have been drifting for quite a long time.

Dearth of successful planning must surely be apparent here and, in addition, a certain irresponsibility towards security in general. Such writers may generate lots of ideas and be most companionable but their general sense of irresponsibility must surely make them a most unsettling influence. To proceed with the 'ship' theory, the bridge is alive with discussion as to where to go next and the passengers are having a wonderful time but below decks the galley is empty and the engines are not functioning...the very next rock is likely to bring about a shipwreck!

Baseline

The baseline is the visible or invisible line upon which writing sits. Assuming that a choice exists, a writer who chooses to use lined writing paper relieves himself of the chore of having to exercise a measure of self-discipline to keep the lines of writing horizontal. But unless the analyst knows that the writer had a choice of paper and chose lined in preference to unlined, no relevance should be attached to the use of lined paper.

Close examination of a writing sample may reveal faint guidelines drawn in by the writer. This phenomenon is of two-fold interest for it reveals not only that the writer was prepared to devote additional time to improving the appearance of his communication, i.e. appearance was as important as content, but also that the writer felt unsure of his own ability to keep the lines of writing on a consistently horizontal plane and recognised the need to utilise a 'crutch', in the form of a guide line, to assist his desired progress.

In handwriting analysis terms, the baseline is the divide between the conscious and the unconscious. The baseline ought to be fairly flexible because it must respond to the rises and falls of desire and instinct. The conscious mind will cause the baseline to lift while the unconscious will cause it to fall.

The horizontal is the shortest and fastest route across the page and is, therefore, the most desirable route.

Extremely straight baseline

I am under control – and how!

To maintain control over their own responses, these writers curb their natural responses and therefore their spontaneity. Vitality level may be high but the writer's self-discipline is rigidly controlling output.

Slightly flexible baseline

I am under control — with reason!

Composed but responsive, this is the ideal balance. If this is maintained throughout a fair sized writing sample, say fifteen lines or more, it may be interpreted as a clear indication that the writer is emotionally stable. In addition, this is a sign of orderliness, perseverance and reasonable self-discipline.

Undulating baseline

I am rather more flexible!

Strongly responsive to outside influence, these writers are striving for equilibrium but the swings are so marked that the attempt to compensate is exaggerated. A strongly undulating baseline is indicative of a moody personality — one with a lot of nervous energy and a flexibility of approach.

Erratic baseline

I am rather unsure as to direction!

The tension between the inner drives and the outer responses is somewhat tortuous. There is indecision in responses and a certain instability of persona.

An erratic baseline is often a temporary feature of writing which materialises when the writer is struggling under an especially heavy burden of stress. If an erratic baseline is a consistent writing feature, it must be regarded in a very negative light. Such writers tend to stray between reality and unreality with abandon and, what is more, without really being aware of the change.

Ascending baseline

This is a sign of ascending aspirations. This is a positive sign which indicates eagerness of approach in a similar way a rising voice mirrors rising emotions. When the first few lines of a letter rise it is an accurate pointer to the fact that the writer embarked upon the letter in a good humour and very probably with a positive twinkle in his eye.

Descending baseline

There are two possibilities here. One is that the writer is unwell, tired or depressed — possibly a combination. Alternatively, instead of the writer not being able to muster enough spirit or strength to keep the line horizontal, descending lines may be quite deliberate and a sign of a rather negative determination. When the latter, descending lines are often accompanied by features indicating resentment, criticism or just sheer non co-operation. Whereas if the former applies and the writer is in a bit of a trough, then the writing will contain more positive signs which will counterbalance the negative trends.

Individual words or short phrases rise

I shall be finished by tomorrow.

When taken in context this is usually regarded as evidence that the writer feels particularly positive towards the word or phrase in question. Evaluate this feature as you would if you heard someone positively emphasise the spoken word or phrase.

Individual words or short phrases fall

I wonder whether Sue will be there?

When taken in context this is usually regarded as evidence that the writer feels particularly negative towards the word or phrase in question. Evaluate this feature as you would if you heard someone negatively emphasise the spoken word or phrase.

Lines fall then rise

It was a miserable day until ...

These writers may start well but they soon begin to lose interest or stamina. Upon realising their predicament they strive and succeed in regaining momentum. If a temporary feature in writing, this may be interpreted as an indication of the writer's battle with and subsequent triumph over a passing handicap such as fatigue. If a consistent feature, then this is indicative of the writer's constant battle with his own rather negative drives. These writers are often their own worst critics!

Lines rise then fall

what a great idea, but won't . . . .

Rising enthusiasm for the task in hand may carry this writer beyond his capacity, resulting in a somewhat predictable waning of both enthusiasm and capability. If form standard is high, the brake on progression will be controlled by the writer. If form standard is low, then the impetus peters out of its own accord. These writers resist taking NO for an answer until they have little option but to do so.

Rising steps

and then she opened the letter and found - - -

The writer is endeavouring to hold his exuberance in check. Although there is evidence of the writer's rising spirits, optimism and ambition, he is enforcing immense self-discipline upon himself to prevent his high spirits revealing themselves.

This is somewhat reminiscent of a small child with an exciting secret whose shining eyes and breathless talk defeat his endeavours to give nothing away!

Falling steps

if only my premium bomd would come up . . . .

The writer is valiantly fighting a downward pull. His stamina, or optimism, is failing but, nevertheless, he is endeavouring to finish the task in hand. Anyone who has indulged in steep hill walking will recognise a heart-pounding, leaden-footed familiarity with this writing feature.

Slant

The action of writing is a repeated progression from left to right. The object being, within a reasonable time, to record thoughts on paper for future reference. Time is an essential component of handwriting analysis. The beginning of a line on the left is older than the end of that same line at the right. Moving away from the left edge of the paper is a beginning; terminating a line of writing at the right side of a page is an ending.

Continuing this train of thought, the left of a page is both a beginning and the past; what is in the process of being written is the present; the right of the page is both an ending and the future. This left to right movement takes place in the horizontal dimension and all progress is in terms of left to right movement. Right to left movement, on the other hand, opposes progression: to achieve the ultimate goal such regressive movement must be controlled and kept to a minimum. Horizontal movement may be taken as a measure of social development and can point to the manner in which a writer tackles day-to-day situations. Communication, emotional expression, sociability, behaviour and choice of objectives are all manifest in this horizontal plane.

Whereas investigation of writing zones will reveal the writer's inner self, the slant is indicative of the outer being. Whether Copybook or unusual, to the right or to the left, the slant of writing will always point towards a writer's inclination for or against an issue.

When achievement is foremost in the writer's mind, every attempt is made to push towards the right. In body language terms leaning forwards is indicative of interest: a person is eager to convince and to be convinced, eager to reach goals, in a hurry — perhaps impatient, perhaps excited. Whatever the motivation, an individual with right slanting writing is rather akin to a runner leaning towards the finishing line.

A push to the left is a contradiction of effort. When involved in a forward manoeuvre why should someone choose to face the direction from whence they came? A desire to cling hold of the past perhaps? The left, being associated with the past, holds a link with a writer's earlier years and therefore memories of childhood, the mother figure, etc. Or may be the writer is exhibiting a reluctance to face the future?

Writing which slants to the right may contain 'left-slanted' movements

and examination of left-slanted writing may reveal 'right-slanted' movements.

The right-slanted writer, by including regressive movements, is exposing conflicts within himself about the future. In general terms this means he is progressing towards the goal in question but once his pen has left the page and the progression is interrupted he expends additional energy in retracing his own steps a little. Such manifestations are often indicative of a writer's feelings of unease or caution about the future — the writer is applying the brakes to steady his progress.

The opposite tendency, which is left-slanted writing that contains some right-tending movement, is the manifestation of positive impulses in an overall negatively inclined manoeuvre...glimmers of hope in an otherwise negative view, perhaps?

The speaker who consistently looks away from his audience is viewed with suspicion. The listener who takes pains to lean away from the person he is listening to is registering lack of interest. The walker who takes one step back for every two steps forwards is impeding his own progress. Anyone who prefers to dwell upon what has been in preference to what may be achieved in the future is exhibiting distinctly negative leanings, to say the least!

'Non-slant', or upright lettering, is indicative of a writer's refusal to allow himself to be swayed into revealing his inclinations. He is exhibiting his independence — the more rigidly he stays upright, the stronger his desire for independence.

The grossly fluctuating slant must be examined closely. The writer's reactions may be erratic: he may be swinging between negative and positive (stop and go) or repression and expression. As many samples of writing as possible should be obtained to ascertain whether this is a temporary feature or a consistent wavering of emotional tides.

Measuring the slant

No choice but to go back to the school room for the humble protractor. The slant of writing is best determined by the measurement of the down strokes in the middle and upper zones. If measuring the angle a loop takes, draw a line from the highest point to where the lines cross at the bottom.

If you take the Copybook slant as the norm you can measure slant as follows: the baseline upon which your protractor is placed must be a real or imaginary horizontal line running from left to right on the page as opposed

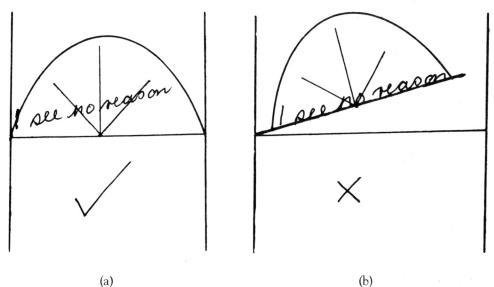

(a)   (b)

to the actual baseline of the writing. The reason for this is demonstrated simply by the diagram on the previous page: normal progression across the page is from left to right rather than from left to upper right. Taking the natural rising baseline (b) as the norm would give an extreme rightward, and totally false, slant, whereas using the 'invisible' baseline of (a) gives the true upright slant (in this case) of the writing.

If you take 1 as the Copybook (see diagram below), fifteen degrees to the right will give +2, thirty degrees to the right will give +3, forty-five degrees will give +4. Conversely, fifteen degrees to the left will give −2, thirty degrees will give −3, forty-five degrees will give −4.

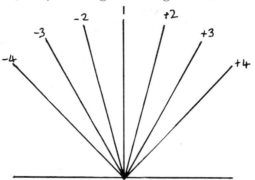

A word of caution, measurements should be made at frequent intervals all over the writing sample, whether or not the slant looks consistent to the eye.

First consider the slant of the left-handed writer whose 'natural' inclination is to the left. Right-handers pull the pen, left-handers push the pen. Right-handers move away from what they are writing, left-handers cover what they are writing. The most comfortable angle for the pen to sit in a left-hander's hand results in the writing having a slope to the left of some 35 to 40 degrees. The question to be asked, therefore, is why so many left-handers choose to curl their wrists and hands around in such a fashion

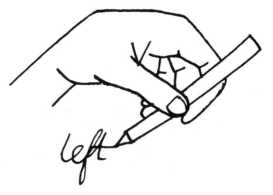

as to produce a slant to the right. I think the answer lies in the fact that writing is hardly the most natural, let alone comfortable, occupation in the world, irrespective of the writer's dominant hand. If so inclined, a slant to the right may be obtained by the left-hander who adjusts the position of his body and the paper.

We cannot disregard 'handedness', but in the final analysis it must be assumed that as every writer is able to adjust his body position to that of the writing surface and the writing instrument, every writer will produce the writing slant that fits his social inclination.

Vertical (−1/+1)

Head tends to rule heart. This individual rarely loses control and if it does happen, control is soon regained. Independent, sometimes to the extent of appearing indifferent, this writer functions well when coolness of temperament is the order of the day. Responses will be cautious humour, dry rather than slap stick.

Slight right slant (+2)

These writers' heads usually rule their hearts but such people are responsive to the needs of others. Although not over-demonstrative they will respond with lively interest once their attention has been caught. Often called the 'normal' slant, this writing reveals an individual's willingness to move away from the norm to achieve his own ends.

Marked right slant (+3)

These writers cannot prevent showing their emotions. Often especially compassionate, they may get carried along by the mood of the moment. Essentially future orientated, they are anxious to progress and give vent to their feelings along the way. These people often make somewhat lively companions.

Extreme slant (+4)

Full speed ahead! Intense reactions. These people do nothing by halves — they will either love to distraction or hate to the ends of the earth. They are often impatient, passionate, impulsive and aggressively motivated. They may become deeply inspired or buoyantly forward thinking; on the other hand, they may become just as deeply wounded or wretchedly deflated. This pace is often too fast to keep up for long and may well be a temporary phenomenon or a prelude to an empty 'shell'.

Any slant away from the direction in which the rest of the writing is heading and which is not a prescribed part of the letter formation must be regarded as a certain 'disinclination' on the part of the writer.

Slightly reclined slant (−2)

On the surface these individuals may be quite outgoing, but this is likely to be nothing more than a facade, a cover-up for inner feelings of inadequacy. These writers may have a deep desire to 'prove' themselves in some remarkable way: they may believe themselves to be different from other people, perhaps because of some special personal gift. They may be a little out of touch with their own anxieties and, as a result, may tend to leave remedial action until circumstances force them to act. They may be harbouring a rather immature reliance upon ideas based around their mother figures and, at the same time, may regard the father figure in a somewhat negative light.

Markedly reclined slant (−3)

The enigmas: these people are self-centred, distance themselves from deep relationships (the mother-figure influence is high) and often opt to live in the past to quite a high degree. Such writers may appear friendly enough but they are usually difficult to understand and, in turn, will resent and resist attempts to understand their inner motivations.

Extremely reclined slant (−4)

Like the +4 writers they are not encountered very often. They identify very, very closely with the past and their mother figure − so closely in fact that their own development has been, to a large extent, suppressed. These writers may appear friendly but all too often are emotionally aloof.

Mixed slant

These people are often subject to wide swings of mood. They are affected strongly by changes in their environment and their emotional reactions are likely to vary according to circumstances. Often undisciplined, they appear to want both to swim with and against the tide at the same time. When mixed slant is a consistent feature of writing over a period of time, such writers are frequently found to be rather unstable in their approaches and unwilling to settle to any one course of behaviour.

If mixed slant is a temporary phenomenon, the most common reason for it is that the writer is faced with making an unwelcome decision. The 'see-sawing' of the slant rather neatly mirrors the fluctuations in the writer's moods.

Pressure

When you contract muscles, you are exerting more strength than when you relax them. To test this all you have to do is clench your fist. You will soon discover that the strength exerted as you do this is far stronger than when you open your fingers.

In handwriting terms pressure equals the degree of force used by the writer. It makes itself apparent in a number of ways which are largely dependent upon the writing implement. For instance, if a nib has been used pressure forces the prongs apart and produces a wider stroke. Light pressure on a nib, on the other hand, results in the prongs staying together and the stroke being narrow.

Pressure on a ball-point pen or other hard point will not cause widening of the stroke but will result in a deeper indentation of the writing surface. Felt-, or other soft-tipped, pens produce an increased depth of ink colour when extra pressure is used and, when the tip is very soft, a widened stroke.

Pencil lines reveal pressure with an increased depth of colour. The gradual widening of pencil strokes is caused by the point wearing down, not increased pressure, and the sudden narrowing of pencil strokes is invariably due to judicious use of an appropriate sharpener. If you do not have access to the original document then pressure will be difficult, if not impossible, to gauge from a copy, regardless of the quality of the copier.

The action of writing involves constant contracting and relaxing of muscles. Upstrokes are 'release' strokes and, as a result, lack the force of downstrokes which are contractions. Not only is the overall pressure in any one pen stroke of interest but also how well the writer is able to maintain or restrain the force used. This control gives an indication of how well the writer is able to utilise whatever energy he has available to him.

At the point of change, where contraction becomes relaxation, if the pressure is seen to be strong it is an indication that the writer has consistency of energy level; whereas if the pressure is weak, it indicates the writer lacks the necessary consistency of energy to enable him to encounter and deal smoothly with changes.

Light pressure

Writing is very much like speech. Quiet speech may spring from a variety of motives; for example, not wishing to draw undue attention to oneself, or perhaps a reluctance to indulge in such indelicate behaviour as loud talking. The same interpretations may be placed upon light pressure in writing. When physical weakness alone is the cause of light pressure a writer may attempt to redress the balance by mustering all available strength to increase pressure, but this invariably fades away. To make a comparison with speech think of an invalid struggling to muster a clear speaking voice, usually in an attempt to emphasise a particular word or sentiment. A sudden loud word in an otherwise weak voice sounds disjointed and makes the listener all the more aware of the speaker's debility.

Consistently light pressure is an indication of a writer's sensitivity. Will-power is not usually very strong and such people are often easily dominated by their more heavy-handed companions. However, if light pressure writing has a high form standard it may be judged as a sign of the writer's high ideals, creative good taste and general fastidiousness.

Medium pressure

Pressure that does not extend into either extreme is a most positive handwriting feature. In healthy, spontaneous writing there ought to be a regularity of increases and decreases of writing pressure. Absolute sameness is abnormal. Equate this with speaking in a monotone — very odd and very artificial. A well modulated speaking voice combines many inflexions into a harmonious whole — just so with well modulated writing.

Heavy pressure

These writers are literally making an impression! This may be a consistent feature of writing or a single attempt to emphasise content. Usually strong willed and assertive, their energy levels are high.

There is a distinction to be made between heavy pressure and excessively heavy pressure. Again, think of speech and consider the difference between the assertive tone of the confident speaker as opposed to the overloud voice of the speaker who is over-compensating in a desperate attempt to be heard.

Heavy pressure with high form standard reveals an assertive writer who is well in control. Heavy pressure with low form standard is indicative of fear, feelings of inadequacy, irritability and tendency towards the irrational.

When extremely heavy pressure occurs it is rarely, if ever, absolutely consistent throughout all the letter forms. Examine the writing closely to determine whether the heaviest pressure is in the vertical (up and down) strokes or the horizontal (side to side) strokes.

If the writing is excessively heavy in the vertical formations, then there is a likelihood that the writer is especially anxious to stand by his principles. He may be self-centred, opinionated and over-ambitious. Such pressure is often a sign of anger and a desire to express it. Sensually preoccupied, these writers may feel a need to make up for their feelings of inadequacy — I *WILL!*

If the writing is excessively heavy in the horizontal formations, then there is reason for concern. The writer is revealing a disparity between his inner drives and his ability to utilise them. Outwardly demonstrative, these people may indulge in verbal haranguing of opponents (often with much fist shaking, etc!) They are aware of their anger but instead of acknowledging that it may stem from within, they tend to believe it is only in response to anger and antagonism from others. If this feature appears in sudden bursts it may well mean that the writer suffers from feelings of paranoia (*YOU* won't!)

Spacing

When faced with a writing surface, the writer is presented with a myriad of choices. Should the writing dominate the entire area? If space is left empty what purpose, if any, could or should the emptiness serve? There are decisions to be made in relation to the margin sizes, the spaces between letters, between words, between lines, and each decision carries its own interpretation.

The page equates with the writer's actual environment. The spaces between letters are an indication of an individual's introversion or extroversion. The spaces left between words reveal the distance the writer keeps between himself and other people. The spaces between the lines of writing measure the gulf between the writer and the expression of his emotions.

To assess the meaning of spacing you must first contemplate the page as a whole. If you half close your eyes until the writing becomes no more than a grey block, the margins surrounding it will serve as a frame around the 'picture' of writing.

To be most pleasing to the eye a picture is framed by spaces on all four sides. The spaces to the left and right should be of equal size while the upper and lower spaces should be slightly larger, the lower space being the largest of all.

Writing margins serve additional purposes to merely ensuring that the writing block is easy on the eye. They make useful receptacles for notes and amendments. When writing is in book form, the inner margins act as necessary barriers between the writing and the bookbinder's staples, thread or glue, while the outer margins prevent the reader's fingermarks and page dog-earing from desecrating the text. In addition to these practical uses, margins also serve to reflect a great deal of a writer's personal tastes and attitude towards his environment in general.

Before mass production began in the mid-1800s, paper was virtually all hand-made and, as a consequence, was a most valuable and scarce commodity. Writers were encouraged to be frugal in their use of paper, so margins tended to be as narrow as possible. Mistakes were costly and did not result in a screwed up ball being tossed into the wastepaper basket — waste paper did not exist. Before the advent of 'liquid paper' writing errors were carefully scratched out or, if the depth of paper did not allow such treatment, the mistake was either written over or crossed out and the corrected word was inserted above the offending item. Even mild scrutiny of many museum-cossetted documents will reveal the tell-tale roughening of paper which was the end result of someone's furtive scratchings.

The utilisation of wood pulp instead of rags to make paper meant the birth of mass production, which in turn brought acres of virgin paper to eager writers. Thus, confronted with the opportunity to indulge in spacing, writers began to exercise artistic licence with a vengeance!

Equate the page with a garden lawn and the writer with the person who pushes the lawn mower. To cut the grass properly (the object of the exercise) the mower must move in even strips from one side to another. As soon as the mower begins its journey the first cut becomes part of the past while the grass which lies ahead remains in the future.

The person mowing has been instructed to leave an uncut area around the mown area to serve as a path (the margin!) Some people will exaggerate the size of the path to make the mown area look that much more special, while more eager mowers in their haste to mow will not feel inclined to waste time or space negotiating the whereabouts of hypothetical paths. Some may begin well but may become bored and start making the paths wider and wider to finish that much sooner, while others may begin untidily but become more disciplined as they get the hang of what they are doing.

The conclusions which can be drawn from the actions of the mower are the same as those of the writer's hand moving across the page.

Margins

Before the 1860s wide margins were a good indication that the writing, or the writer, was of such importance that its value transcended the cost of the paper. Wide margins after the 1860s, however, carry quite a different interpretation.

All margins wide

Often possessing a high level of aesthetic taste, the writer is exhibiting an awareness of the importance of his surroundings. Such writers often

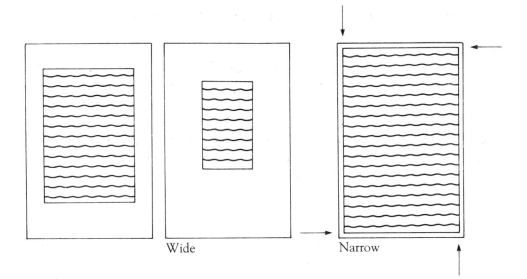

Wide   Narrow

endeavour to surround themselves with a cocoon of material comfort. There is a certain element of aloofness in the person's attitude towards other people and the environment in general — perhaps best described as a somewhat 'touch-me-not' stance.

All margins non-existent

If the writing predates the 1860s it must be remembered that paper was a rather luxurious commodity then and frugality tended to be the order of the day. On the other hand, the modern writer may have had only one piece of paper to write upon; alternatively, if writing is on air-mail paper, it may have been crammed in in an effort to minimise the letter weight. If it is possible to discount the previous three possibilities, a writer's elimination of margins is an indication of his desire to eliminate barriers between himself and the outside world. He may be effusive in speech and obtrusive in manner, and could have a fear or dislike of empty spaces, including the contemplation of the ultimate empty space — death.

Wide left-hand margin

This may be in deference to a book-binding process that would swallow up space to the left. If binding is not envisaged, a wide left-hand margin signifies that the writer is eager to move away from his beginning and in so doing to leave the past behind. This writing feature is often an indication of a high awareness of culture and an eagerness to face the future.

Uneven left-hand margin

A sure sign of a lack of adherence to fixed regulations. This feature may also indicate an inner lack of harmony, resulting in somewhat erratic behaviour.

Left margin widening

A sign of increasing impatience to proceed. If exaggerated, this may indicate an overly optimistic person whose desire to 'get on' with things drives him to leave other matters undone.

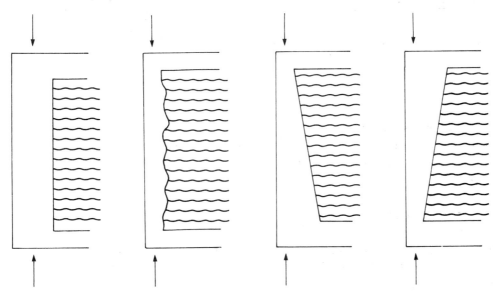

Variations of left-hand margin

Left margin narrowing

The writer has become increasingly aware of his own haste and is attempting to 'back-pedal'. A sudden spate of writing out time tables or lists points to the same realisation of a need to adhere to a fixed framework. The writer is being drawn back to his beginnings.

Narrow margin on left and right sides

A certain lack of reserve is evident here. The writer is deliberately attaching little importance to the traditional barriers and is awarding

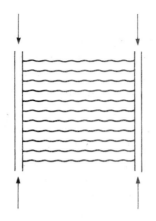

himself increased space at their expense. This may be a sign of a certain lack of consideration towards others.

Wide right-hand margin
The writer is attempting to avoid moving forwards; this may be because of a fear of the future or perhaps the result of great inner reserve or self-discipline.

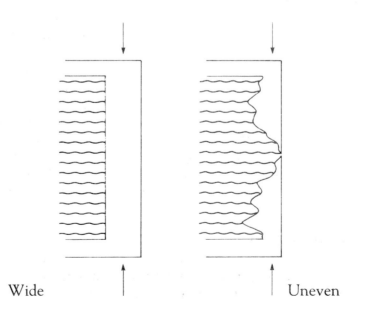

Wide   Uneven

Uneven right-hand margin

An absolutely even right-hand margin is an immensely difficult feat to achieve; a reasonable undulation can be expected because of the difference between the location at which the writer wishes to stop and the word length which permits the stop to take place.

The more uneven the margin, the stronger the emphasis on the following interpretation. The writer has a certain ambivalent attitude towards progress, alternating between spontaneity and self-discipline. There are indications of impulsiveness, possibly making it difficult to predict his reactions in a given circumstance. If a line of writing sometimes extends to the very edge of the paper, the writer is exhibiting a penchant for erratic time-keeping or, in grass-mowing terms, the mower sometimes neglects to look ahead and, as a result, hits the garden fence!

Even right-hand margin

As all words and letters are not of precisely the same size it follows that few lines of writing will be precisely the same size. Most writers make the decision of where to finish a line of writing during the process of completing the last two words. The final result is governed largely by the space left in front of the last word and the number of letters which make up that word.

Compressing letters or splitting words are frowned upon in the school room to such an extent that they materialise only rarely and usually on occasions when haste is uppermost in the writer's mind. They may be interpreted as a sign of poor planning and, if they appear frequently in a sample, as a writer's preference to take the most convenient rather than the correct solution to a problem.

When the right-hand margin is extremely even and no compression, or splitting of words, has taken place the writer is exhibiting immense discipline and skill at forward planning. The price the writer pays for such virtues is a virtual blocking of spontaneous expression. Great self-control is necessary to achieve a straight right-hand margin and such writers are often equally controlled in their emotional responses. The only exceptions to this are writers whose sense of timing is so precise that they 'keep in step' with the margin without much conscious effort — dancers and musicians for example.

Right-hand margin widening

When the amount of writing becomes less and the margin widens, the end of the page is inevitably reached that much sooner. This is usually a reflection of the writer's desire to desist from writing.

Widening   Narrowing

Right-hand margin narrowing

When the amount of writing increases and the margin has to shrink to accommodate it, this is a reflection of the writer's increased enthusiasm for communication.

Wide upper margin

This writer respects formality and tradition. The increased expanse of space before communication begins is a mark of deference — tantamount to a bow or a curtsey — to the person to whom the letter is addressed.

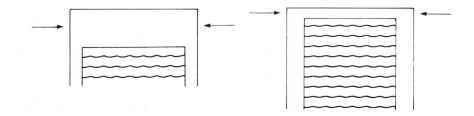

Narrow upper margin

This writer favours informality and directness of approach. A certain indifference towards tradition is indicated and when the narrowness of margin is extreme the sheer bluntness of the beginning points to the writer having taken an obtrusive stance at the onset of the communication. This demolition of traditional barriers could indicate eagerness to communicate and may also be interpreted as carrying slightly pugnacious undertones.

Wide lower margin

The writer has decided to terminate communication on completion of all important messages rather than attempting to fill in the remaining space with chit chat. There is a certain aloofness in this action; the writer is decisive and avoids time wasting even though his actions make him appear rather abrupt.

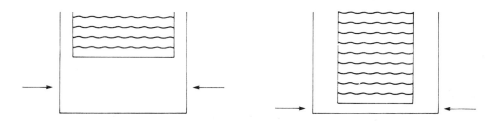

Narrow lower margin

The writer has permitted his communication to be terminated by lack of paper rather than by his own decision to end. There are a number of likely interpretations here which include sentimentality, effusiveness, depression and meanness! (There is also the possibility that there is no more paper; this can be tested by looking at more than one sample to deduce whether the feature is consistent to the writer.)

Spacing between lines

The space left between two lines serves to ensure that upper and lower loops do not entangle with each other, and is thus an important aid to legibility. The amount of space left is a guide to a writer's clarity of thought and also measures the amount of interplay he desires between himself and his general environment.

   Normal spacing on unlined paper will vary but the changes should be both harmonious and slight!

Wide spaces between lines

This writer tends to withdraw from close contact with all but a few people. He may harbour a somewhat inflated view of his own importance *or*

and in the event

he really ought not

practical experience may have taught him to fear closeness. Such a feature is frequently found in the writing of media superstars or the immensely rich, both of whom are likely to fear a surfeit of close contact for obvious reasons.

Narrow spaces between lines

Such a feature is usually produced at speed. The writer is likely to be full of nervous energy, thoughts and ideas tumbling out one on top of the other, resulting in a jumble.

A burst of extreme enthusiasm could cause this feature, but if poor spacing is consistent it should be viewed in a negative light. The more the lines tangle, the more the writer's thoughts are mixed up. The writer's motivation is to pour his feelings out rather than to express them in a way that can be understood.

Variable spaces between lines

and in the event
he really ought not

to have done what

Come here, go away! Variable spacing is often a sign of inconsistency in a writer's social self. Sudden changes from friendliness to apparent hostility may take place. Such writers tend to be subjective and rather confused and changeable in their attitude to the accepted boundaries of sociability. Self-centredness is a trait often discovered in such writers.

Rigidly regular spacing between lines

and in the event he really

ought not to have done what

he did, especially when one

Writing is the sum total of the interaction between writing surface, the environment, human muscle, sinew and tendon, imagination, experience, motivation and the writing implement. It is *never* rigid in formation unless immense control is exercised by the writer. The more control, the less the spontaneity of expression. The fact that a writer feels a need to curb his spontaneity is a signpost to his fearing the outcome should he relax and thus lose control of self or his immediate environment.

Spacing between words

The average space between words should be about the width of a small letter 'w'. This space is not fixed and will vary according to the letters at each side. The space left between words symbolises the distance the writer wishes to keep between himself and society. This is the writer's own personal space and indicates his need for close proximity with others or, alternatively, his desire to keep other people at arm's length.

Very narrow spaces between words

cometoseemesoon

This writer craves companionship. He obtains emotional sustenance from close relationships and, in turn, fears loneliness. If the narrownesss is extreme, this is an indication that the writer is selfish in his demands for attention. Such a feature frequently appears in the writing of 'media people', especially those personalities who thrive on ego boosts and applause from their admirers.

Very wide spaces between words

come   to   see

Wide spaces between words are a sign of a writer's desire for isolation. This often stems from a need for a certain amount of privacy in an otherwise crowded lifestyle, but may also indicate an inability or unwillingness to communicate with others, resulting in a withdrawal from society.

Extremely variable spacing between words

This is an unusual feature and would indicate a high level of relationship insecurity. The writer wants company and yet does not really trust or rely upon companionship. Either immaturity or anxiety is likely to be a contributory factor to such inconsistency.

Spacing within words

To assess inner word spacing, both letter width and connecting stroke width must be taken into joint consideration.

Letter width

A single letter form represents, in many ways, the writer's view of himself. A tight, narrow formation indicates a self-conscious, rather ungenerous, attitude towards his own needs and desires; whereas a relaxed, broad letter form reveals that the writer is relaxed and generous in relation to his own requirements.

Connection stroke width

The distance between letters links directly with the way the writer relates to other people. Letters that are placed close together, often virtually jostling each other, indicate introversion while widely spaced letters indicate extroversion.

Letter width combined with connection stroke width

It does not necessarily follow that a wide, relaxed letter form will be joined to its fellows by wide, relaxed connecting strokes:

Wide letter, wide connection This writer is outgoing. He views his own persona with pleasure and is unafraid of making outside contacts.

Wide letter, narrow connection This writer is at ease with his view of himself but is self-centred and demanding in his dealings with others.

Narrow letter, wide connection This writer is likely to appear relaxed and outgoing but in reality he views self with some disquiet and may be both self-conscious and very self-critical.

Narrow letter, narrow connection This writer is introverted; he relates all inner sensations and outer events back to his own ego. Such writers are often discontented, unhappy people who fail to make much progress with realising their aspirations.

Connections and letter shapes

Fluidity of writing reflects the smooth flow of the writer's thinking processes, mental abilities and personal presentation.

It stands to reason that a word which is written with a single pen movement should take little time and effort to write, whereas a word which is made up of several unconnected pen movements ought to require the expenditure of more time and effort. Some writers endeavour to minimise disconnections by joining whole words together while others may resist connecting letters to the extent of writing each separately. There are many and varied degrees of 'connectedness': to assess their meanings correctly careful observation must be applied so that both the writer's intent and actual achievement may be ascertained.

After laying a piece of tracing paper over the sample, trace the writing with an *empty* ball-point pen. The action of retracing the writer's movements will reveal the flow or lack of it in the writing. Disconnections may actually speed the flow when the alternative is an ungainly Copybook formation. The writer may even have incorporated time-consuming connections in an effort to embellish or exhibit his cleverness.

A good speaking voice is judged by its pleasing qualities and its clear audibility. Good writing is recognised in a similar way, i.e. when it is both visually pleasing *and* easily legible. Seemingly clever or ornate letter shapes and time-consuming or illogical disconnections serve only to impair legibility and should be judged in a distinctly negative light!

Connected writing

I like to join things

70

When most, though not necessarily all, of the letters in a word are joined together the writing is deemed to be connected.

As a general rule of thumb, connected writing is favoured by those whose thought processes are logical and goal-orientated. Such writers wish to complete what they start and endeavour to proceed with whatever they are doing according to a preconceived plan of action.

Sometimes 'connected' writers become so enmeshed with maintaining an overall theme that they overlook the smaller and apparently less relevant aspects of everyday life. As a result they may appear inconsiderate towards the finer feelings of some of the more sensitive among us. Connected writers become bored unless they have a goal to work towards. Even their leisure time is likely to consist of completing, solving and improving things.

When the 'connectedness' is so complete that whole words are connected, the writer is revealing a strong leaning towards the use of pre-planned strategy. These people are all too often extremely difficult to distract once they have embarked upon a plan of campaign. Objectivity is the rule of their day and attempts to sway their feelings tend to be shrugged aside. They are often found in careers which require a high level of applied judgement. High intelligence is frequently found in such writers.

Disconnected writing

I certainly do not

The fewer the connections, the more strongly the attributes of disconnected writing apply. Occasional breaks occur in most writing and serve to simplify the otherwise pedantic Copybook writing style. Constant disconnection diminishing writing speed requires more effort to execute.

'Disconnected' writers are revealing a tendency to view a word as a collection of letters rather than as one whole. In a negative light this may be described as being unable 'to see the wood for the trees' and indeed disconnected writers do tend to think on an individual basis rather than in specific themes. Such writers are intuitive and reach decisions aided by the way they feel at the time rather than by logical deduction.

Open, as they are, to impression and the mood of the moment such writers are often subjective in their thinking and are easily diverted from the train of thought they were following at the time the diversion occurred. Disconnected writers are great justifiers of their own actions and, as a result, tend to resist looking at themselves in a critical light. Often creative and sometimes possessing an amazing depth of insight they can, nevertheless, be irritatingly inconsistent and devastatingly insecure.

Printed lower case writing

I hope you understand

Printed writing is often favoured by people who encountered trouble in learning to write. Alternatively, the writer who feels unsure as to the ability of his reader to understand his writing may decide that simplification by printing will serve to enhance legibility.

If the writer did not encounter trouble in learning to write and is not temporarily adopting a simplistic style, then rather different conclusions may be reached when consistently printed handwriting is analysed.

'Printed' writers are often loners who resist many of the accepted social mores to the extent of being rebellious or even anti-social. These writers are often very ambitious and competitive as well as rather introverted, leading to their wanting to do things in their own way but then, as a result, feeling themselves to be isolated. Co-operation with team goals is often difficult for them to achieve as they tend to be aloof and critical within relationships.

Writing in capitals

THIS IS MY WAY OF DOING

If consistent to the writer, this writing tendency is an indication of extreme self-centredness. This is often a sign of immaturity and an inability to adapt behaviour to a given occasion. If equated with speaking, the writer is addressing everyone he encounters in a loud, slow voice — appropriate to deaf, stupid or ignorant people, but inappropriate to normal communication: 'DO YOU UNDERSTAND?'

Erratic combination of writing and printing

actually I HoPE you will COmE

Extreme anxiety is evident in such writing, resulting in confusion and inconsistency of behaviour. The overall interpretation is one of instability and emotional turmoil.

A printed word or phrase in an otherwise cursive sentence

Whereas an underlining indicates that the word in question is of special importance, printing it tends to give it a negative impact, e.g. whereas 'we *do* hope he brings his mother' implies that his mother will be a welcome guest, 'we DO hope he brings his mother' strikes an odd note and makes the reader wonder exactly what it is about his mother that makes her an object of such interest. Sarcasm is often expressed in this way. By such over-exaggeration the writer is actually divorcing himself from the particular word.

Disconnected cursive writing

how kind

These writers frequently find difficulty in extending the hand of friendship. They may well be friendly enough but do not seem able to grasp the implications of society's niceties; for instance, it may not occur to such a writer to return an invitation to a friend who has extended such an invitation to him. These writers may not be mean but can appear to be so, because unless asked they will not give. Their behaviour is often repetitive and they do not seem able to adapt their behaviour to suit specific situations.

Other people's behaviour within relationships may perplex such writers as they find real difficulty in seeing a situation from another person's standpoint.

Artistic printing

AND SO WE proceed...

These writers have constructed their writing in such a way for it to appear particularly legible and aesthetically appealing. Artists, architects and some engineers do this when excellence of presentation transcends the desire to appear spontaneous.

Letter connections and shapes
Copybook connections and letters are made up of four basic shapes.

uu write
Garland

mm write
Arcade

m write
Angle

— write
Thread

It is the predominance of one or perhaps two of these formations that enables conclusions to be drawn.

Garland connections and shapes

under uu

Predominantly garland letter forms indicate an open, responsive personality. Rarely strongly competitive or aggressive, these writers usually opt to maintain the status quo rather than inaugurate change. Garland connections often point to great sentimentality.

Shallow garland

under uu

Shallow garlands indicate a personality which prefers to take the easiest route on every occasion. Often impulsive and sometimes thoughtless, these writers may be easy-going but they do not contribute very heavily to a relationship.

Extremely deep garlands

under uv

These garlands are somewhat overdone and indicate a distinctly subservient tendency in the writer. Hostility is rarely expressed openly as the writer is usually too busy concentrating on being humble and self-abasing.

Arcade connections and shapes

over mn

Predominant arcades are a sign that the writer is guarded, determined and accepts changes only if they are introduced gradually. Status is often carried well by these writers but their lack of openness can result in their motivations being either unknown or misinterpreted − which probably suits their love of intrigue admirably.

Shallow arcades

over ~~

This is a negative writing feature and indicates a tendency in the writer to wish to cover his tracks. Evasiveness, caution and austerity are present to an alarming extent. Great attention should be devoted to scrutinising this writer's motivating forces.

Extremely high or exaggerated arcades

over Wh

Such exaggerations are akin to the theatrical appearance or gestures of the showman. Attention is being drawn away from the reality towards 'tinsel'.

These writers may be compensating for an inferiority complex by showing off.

Angled connections and shapes

straight mm

Logic, precision and idealism are revealed by the angle. Positively, these writers favour accuracy and determination. Negatively, they may be inflexible and may ruthlessly seek to impose their will upon others.

Extremely angular

straight mm

If combined with heavy pressure, this is a sign of anger which is released physically. Hostility is evident and applying the force of his will is to the forefront of this writer's intentions.

Erratic angularity

if your son calls

When a word or phrase is written in an angular fashion and the body of the writing is not, the writer is endowing the word or phrase with an aggressive emphasis. (The heavier the writing pressure the higher the blood pressure!) If increased angularity appears erratically and not in any particular word, the writer is finding difficulty in disciplining and understanding his own reactions and drives. If pressure is equally erratic, this combination is a distinct danger signal as it points to ungoverned aggression.

Thread connections and shapes

at the speed of

Threads are not taught but are born out of speed of writing. The hand endeavouring to follow the brain speed has sacrificed some of the legibility. If the threads are rhythmical and the writing still attains legibility, then a positive interpretation can be made. Such writers are usually sensitive and creative. Often intuitive and intensely observant, they frequently have links with one or more branches of the Arts. Threaded writers resist being labelled and often consider themselves to be somewhat free spirits.

Threads which result in illegibility must be interpreted negatively, as these writers are openly revealing their inability to communicate either their desires or their knowledge. They are often difficult to understand (in more ways than one!) They can be capricious, impatient and disorganised. Frequently eccentric, they manage to go entirely their own way but their lack of foresight may well result in their getting lost.

Threads at word endings

Provided that the threading does not destroy legibility, this is often an indication of the writer's negotiating and mediating abilities. Such writers are very astute and can see what lies behind other people's facades without disturbing their own. This is a sign of a high level of applied intelligence.

Threads at the end of a writing sample
When writing undergoes a gradual process of disintegration, resulting in increased threading as the sample progresses, it is a sure sign of the writer's fading interest and subsequent eagerness to come to the end. Such writers are often easily bored and will approximate what they are doing to finish all the sooner.

Threads in the middle of words

These writers are striving to maintain an outward appearance of competence but their inner resources are being stretched to the limit. If maintained for any real length of time, the outer veneer is very likely to crumble.

Threads at the beginning of words

Extreme hesitation and ambiguity of response is indicated. There is a strong likelihood of mental aberration of some description.

Erratic or occasional threads

May well be a sign of very creative, impressionable thought processes. Such writers are often original thinkers but difficult to pin down. Responses are inconsistent; capriciousness and indecision are combined as the writer strives to remain 'free'.

Beginnings and endings

Whether writing a book or cleaning out a fish tank, organised people who are inclined to 'get ready' beforehand will do so — and people who are not inclined towards preparation will obviously not!

When finishing a project, the decisive individual's ending will be more clearcut than the indecisive person's...and so it is with writing.

Beginnings: examples and explanations

Absence of lead-in stroke — has a directness of approach.

Lead-in on capital letters — has a great sense of occasion; wants to get things *just right!*

Long lead-in — opts for prior preparation; a plotter.
Lead-in from upper zone — likes to exhibit intellect.

Arcade lead-in from upper zone — has imagination.

Angle lead-in from upper zone — has sharp intellect.

Garland lead-in from upper zone — has social intelligence. Lead-in from lower zone — has tense aggression stemming from formative years.

yes Garland lead-in from lower zone — has guilt feelings.

yes Arcade lead-in from lower zone — hides guilt.

yes Angle lead-in from lower zone — blames others.

yes Garland lead-in — is warm, caring, emotional.

yes Long garland lead-in — is warm, caring, emotional, demonstrative.

yes Drooping garland lead-in — a time-waster.

yes Arcade lead-in — secretive, defensive, resists 'telling-all'!

yes Angle lead-in — hostility, resentment stemming from past.

yes Thread lead-in — uncertainty, indecision.

yes Long thread lead-in — has a flexible approach but time-wastes and distorts past facts.

yes Hooked lead-in — refuses to let go of past.

yes   Very small hook on lead-in − passing irritation.

Endings: examples and explanations

Distinct endings (any formation) − energy does not easily dissipate.

now

No endings − directness, abruptness, has clearcut attitude to life.

Exaggeratedly prolonged endings − determination, generosity, possessiveness, is security minded.

now we will

Endings uplifted − spiritual leanings, high standards, seeks higher order.

now we will

Endings vertically upward − maintains front, secretive, imaginative.

now we will

Endings left and up − self-orientated, seeks protection.

now we will

Endings left and cutting through word − introverted, self-critical.

now we will

Endings left and down − anti-social, refuses compromise (would rather argue).

now we will

Endings short and heavy − energetic, abrupt.

now we will

Endings long and heavy — energetic, stubborn, angry.

now we will

Endings long and sharp — sharp-tongued, opinionated.

now we will

Endings vertically downwards — lack of compromise, decisive, intolerant.

now we will

Incomplete endings — curt, would rather curtail proceedings than compromise or negotiate.

now we will

Endings up and with right extension — pretentious, indirect, will deliberately confuse the issue.

now we will

Thread endings — hasty, lacks attention to detail, anxious to finish.

now we will

Angle endings — abrupt, aggressive, disciplined.

now we will

Garland endings — talkative, sociable, responsive (dislikes goodbyes).

now we will

Arcade endings — secretive, cautious, does not reveal everything.

now we will

Flourished endings — theatrical, enjoys creating drama.

now we will

Many different endings — has a flexible attitude (other traits will determine direction).

Specific letter formations

By examining specifics it is possible to determine many fascinating little idiosyncrasies which add colour to a personality profile. But be warned — *critics of Graphology find particular satisfaction in ridiculing so-called personality assessments apparently based on the occasional pen twitch* (as likely to stem from a wobbly table leg as from the inner core of the writer's being) *and deliberate elaborations which anyone with an iota of rudimentary knowledge of writing could incorporate in their writing* (done probably to trip up an unwary handwriting analyst).

Unfortunately many would-be handwriting analysts assist the sceptics by falling headlong into the trap of setting far too much store by specifics (probably because they are quick and easy to spot!) and then, as a result, making stupid and often dangerous mistakes.

There are publications aplenty which are comprised mainly, if not entirely, of letter specifics and their possible interpretation. These are fine, as far as they go, but whether professional or amateur, no handwriting analyst worth consideration refers to specifics until *after* the main body of the analysis is complete.

To put the record straight — a detailed and accurate analysis may be obtained without *any* reference to specifics.

If, since the beginning of writing, everyone in the world had been taught to write in the same way and according to the same Copybook style, then specifics would have been awarded a more important place in analysis. Time and distance cause massive differences in Copybook writing: a 'curly-twirly' specific formation would be seen as gross elaboration in some writing styles whereas such a formation might be nothing more than a mundane example of Copybook in another sample.

The specifics that analysts *should* pay attention to are i dots, t bars, lower case d's and g and y lower loops. But even these features must first be checked as far as possible to deduce the Copybook norm.

There are also some rule-of-thumb measurements which may safely be referred to when considering specific capital or lower case letters. After testing these specifics you will find that you are able to add more of your own, each according to the Copybook style in question.

The i dot

In many ways similar to the placement of the t bar, the i dot is an interruption in the writing flow. Most writers do not dot the i until they have written the entire word. To minimise the break in writing flow the dot is often 'thrown' into place by a fast leftward movement, the writer being more anxious to move on to the next word than to devote much time or effort to the exact placement of such an insignificant (seemingly) item.

Examples

Pressure lighter than stem — writer is especially fastidious, sensitive, weak or unassertive.

Pressure heavier than stem — writer is emphatic, perhaps obtrusive.

Left of stem — (an over-compensation) writer is cautious, shy or fearful.

Right of stem — writer anticipates the next action (impulsive perhaps?)

High placement — writer has lots of imaginative drive. If pressure is light, the writer may well have a leaning towards spirituality.

Placement average height — writer favours method, order and discipline.

Placement low — writer endowed with good concentration and memory.

Placement below top point of stem — writer is fearful, cautious or repressed.

No dot (first check whether this is a high placed dot hiding in the previous line of writing) — writer is careless or preoccupied, resulting in absent-mindedness.

Acute accent — writer has a lively, original mind.

Grave accent — writer has a well honed critical sense.

Sharpened accent — sarcastic.

Clubbed accent — emphatic; if very heavy, aggressive.

Shapely(!) — has a lively humour, sense of fun.

Circle (or other drawn shape) — writer is prepared to devote time to creating a desired appearance. If high form level writing, this indicates artistic inclinations. If form level is low, then the writer is trying hard to appear different (a bit of a poseur?)

Joined to another letter — has a high level of logic and expertise in employing own judgement.

t bars

Pressure

Bar lighter than stem — sensitive, withdrawn, shy.

Bar heavier than stem — domineering, has strong will power, energetic.

Heavy, becoming light — sharp witted, perhaps sarcastic.

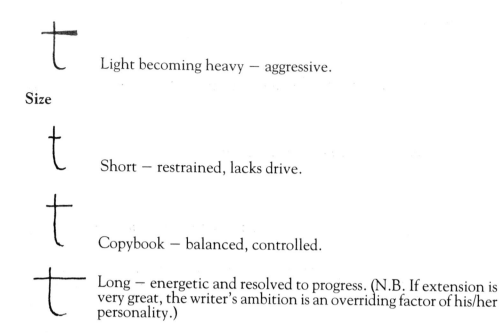

Light becoming heavy — aggressive.

Size

Short — restrained, lacks drive.

Copybook — balanced, controlled.

Long — energetic and resolved to progress. (N.B. If extension is very great, the writer's ambition is an overriding factor of his/her personality.)

Angle

Rising — enthusiastic, has drive, rising spirits.

Falling — despondent, resigned, weak.

Falling with heavy pressure — destructive, aggressive, has negative ambition.

Position

Position on stem denotes the writer's drive toward goals, i.e. high, medium, low, mixed.

Top or above stem – ambition may go 'over the top'.

Left – over-compensates, is cautious.

Right – enthusiastic, has drive, is forward-thinking.

Uncrossed – careless, preoccupied resulting in absent-mindedness; if consistently uncrossed, then the writer is exhibiting bloody-mindedness!

Shape of bar

Triangle – obstinate, determined, outspoken.

Looped – has pride in own or loved one's achievements, joie de vivre, is materialistic.

Knotted – determined, accurate, logical and persistent.

Hill – repressed passions.

Valley – masochistic, evasive.

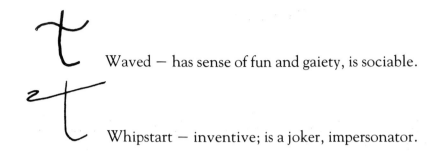

Waved — has sense of fun and gaiety, is sociable.

Whipstart — inventive; is a joker, impersonator.

Shape of stem

Vertical line without crossing — absent-minded or preoccupied. If consistent, has difficulty in communication.

Looped with crossing — writer needs emotional support, enjoys flattery.

Looped without crossing — undisciplined over-reaction; doesn't follow through initial action.

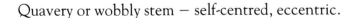

Quavery or wobbly stem — self-centred, eccentric.

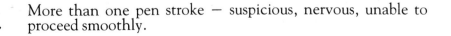

More than one pen stroke — suspicious, nervous, unable to proceed smoothly.

The letter 'd'

High retraced stem — independent, favours understatement, respects spiritual values.

Low retraced stem — independent, shrewd, but if exceptionally short, ego is lacking.

Looped stem — the more inflated the stem, the greater the writer's vanity.

Non-looped stem — manifests good taste.

High, widely looped stem — arrogant.

High, widely looped stem with pointed top — arrogant, isolated, fends others off.

Spread stem — obstinate, over-estimates own capabilities.

 'Greek' formation — writer places much emphasis on reason and excellence, has literary interests.

 Open body — talkative.

 Body clinging on side of stem — obstinate: 'my will be done' attitude.

 Looks like a musical note — has a connection with, or love for, music.

 Top of stem swings to right — is fun loving.

 Connection from left to top of stem — rebellious against accepted norms.

Stem leaning to right against writing flow — over-reacts, is prone to sudden outbursts.

Circular stem enclosing letter body — extremely self-protective, is neurotic and has repetitive habits.

Body open at bottom — extremely negative sign — writer consciously and unconsciously provokes others (will 'cut off nose to spite face'!)

Lower loops

Open 'loop' — unrealistic, unfulfilled.

'Loop' ending in tick — impatient, frustrated.

Deep, full loop — indicative of physical release of energy, emphasis upon satisfaction.

Loop pulled to left — links with mother figure maintained, links with feminine rather than masculine traits (possible teapotical tendencies).

Stick formation — simplistic, dislikes and avoids elaboration.

Long heavy stick — determined and aggressive (linked with defensiveness).

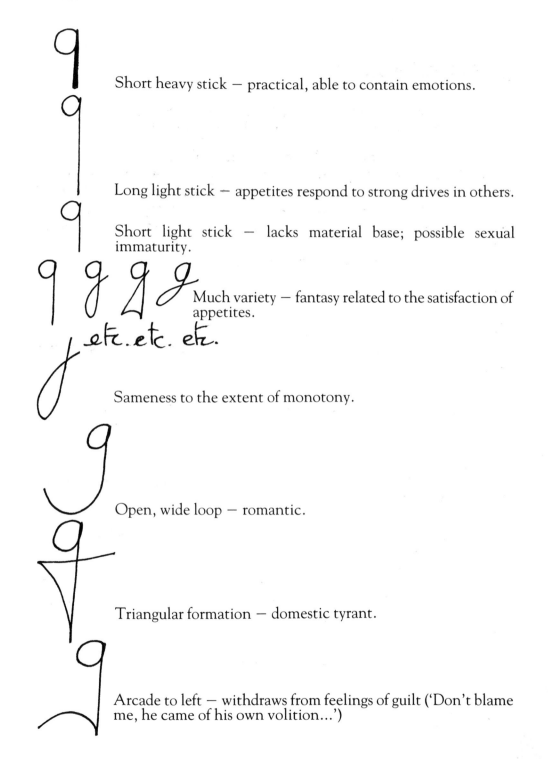

Short heavy stick — practical, able to contain emotions.

Long light stick — appetites respond to strong drives in others.

Short light stick — lacks material base; possible sexual immaturity.

Much variety — fantasy related to the satisfaction of appetites.

Sameness to the extent of monotony.

Open, wide loop — romantic.

Triangular formation — domestic tyrant.

Arcade to left — withdraws from feelings of guilt ('Don't blame me, he came of his own volition...')

yourself

Zone ends right, with little emphasis on its own importance — suppresses inner drives to achieve other goals.

Capital and lower case generalities

Capital letters always signify a beginning; they are equivalent to a writer making an entrance. There is often elaboration or emphasis of size of capital letters which is not seen anywhere else in the writing sample...and, indeed, most people will concentrate their energy or make an effort as they begin something.

Assessment of likely Copybook norm must be made.

Copybook letter — respects tradition.

Cm Beginning with large loop — needs to attract attention, showman of sorts.

And Printed — desires enhanced communications, dislikes over-elaboration.

Love Swinging formation — characteristic of easy bodily movements, easy charm.

m w Rising top — ambitious, desires to proceed (preferably upwards).

m w Falling top — has to 'lean down' to communicate. Positively, a generous avoidance of protocol; negatively, a 'holier than thou' attitude.

B m Narrow — self-conscious, inhibited.

B S Wide — uninhibited.

95

Excessively loopy or 'ornamental' — vain, has a great sense of occasion.

Structured — constructive, prefers to get to the point, has a direct approach.

Lead-in from lower zone — materialistic, needs security, has links with past.

Lead-in from upper zone — emphasises own intellect.

Separate strokes — is the odd-man-out, distant, has a disjointed approach.

Lower case letters will vary in formation for reasons other than pure personality traits. For instance, the ending of the preceding letter and the beginning of the following letter will contribute greatly to certain changes in formation.

nice = i, noise = i

pit = i, pick = i

Changes or deviations in formation if seen only rarely should *not* be given emphasis within the analysis.

Open top — generous, frank; if extreme, talkative (perhaps overly so!)

σ Knotted top — secretive, cautious.

Ω *big*   Open bottom — exhibits anti-social behaviour.

Δ ρ Knotted bottom — secretive, cautious.

8 9 Similarity to number shapes — quick thinking, has good judgement.

$g^{x}\ell$ Reversed — confused.

and   Looped within body — shrewd, appreciation directed within.

pl fl   Looped or extended into upper zone — shows indpendence of spirit, ambition.

$\mathcal{M}$ Pointed tops — needle-sharp mind, fast.

$\mathcal{UU}$ Pointed tops with very rounded bottoms — sharp-minded but has a yielding nature, resulting in a tendency to under-achieve.

$\Lambda\Lambda$ Pyramid tops — enjoys digging for knowledge.

97

m, n, p Round tops — careful and possesses creative logic.

m, n, p Blunted round tops — lacks intellectual edge, will follow rather than lead, but has a mule-like attitude to change of direction.

Coiling — shrewd, cunning.

The signature and the personal pronoun 'I'

Both the signature and the personal pronoun 'I' represent Self. The difference between the two is that the writer's public self is illustrated by his signature whereas his private self is symbolised by his 'I'.

The reasoning behind this conclusion is very straightforward. When a person puts his full signature to a document the action is essentially formal rather than informal. When writing to a friend or close relation the barriers of formality have been demolished as seen by the way the writer abbreviates his or her signature. The degree of informality is not difficult to judge; for instance, my own full name comprises Diane Mary Simpson. I use my full name only upon legal or other extremely formal documentation. I would use abbreviated forms of my first names, i.e. D.M. Simpson or Diane M. Simpson, on formal letters rather than documents calling for full identification, the relevance being that the signature is that of a Simpson and the name or initials serve to identify which Simpson.

My most commonly used signature is written without my middle name which I omit because of dislike, i.e. Diane Simpson.

Diane Simpson

When corresponding with a friend or relative I am writing not as a Simpson but as Diane, therefore the Simpson goes unless I know that the person to whom I write knows more than one Diane, in which case I either bracket Simpson or abbreviate to a single 'S'.

Diane (Simpson)

Diane S.

I have a pet name known only to very close family (I refuse point blank to reveal what it is!) that I would only use as a signature in moments of intimacy.

I do not choose to incorporate Ms, Mrs or Miss in my signature unless I am specifically required to do so. The fact that my signature includes an obviously female name points to my gender; my marital status is, however, as far as my identity is concerned, largely incidental. In the unlikely event of my choosing to sign my name as D. Simpson then, and only then, would I add Mrs to the signature...and even then I would bracket it and put it at the end.

Most people follow a similar path of graduated informality of signature depending upon their relationship with or attitude towards the person to whom they are writing. Therefore it follows that a full signature is indicative of at least a fairly high level of formality. A signature accurately portrays a writer's public self-image for the person with whom he corresponds.

The personal pronoun 'I' cannot be abbreviated and signifies the writer's private view of self. 'I' can, however, be made more formal by being transformed into the royal 'we' or alternatively being linked to another phrase, e.g. 'my husband and I'.

Both signature and personal pronoun 'I' should be compared with each other as well as with the rest of the writing to assess correctly the writer's private and public self-image.

The signature

Size of signature

To ascertain the size of a signature three comparative measurements with the preceding writing must be made. First, compare the height of the capital letters in the signature with other capitals. If the signature capitals are *larger*, then the writer's public image has an emphasis upon tradition and formality. If the signature capitals are *smaller*, then the writer's public image has an emphasis upon spontaneity and informality.

The second measurement concerns the height of the middle zone letters, i.e. a, c, e, i, m, n, o, r, s, u, v, w and x. If the signature middle zone letters are *larger*, then the writer is trying to draw attention to his public image. Such signatures are usually indicative of a writer's self-confidence and ambition. The larger the signature, the louder the trumpet is blown. It is often an interesting exercise to compare the size of a signature with the size the writer gives to the name of the person he is addressing.

Dear Mr Smith
yours Mr Jones

Equal size implies equal status.

A signature larger than the recipient's name points directly to the importance awarded by the writer to himself.

A signature smaller then the recipient's name is an obvious mark of deep respect but if exaggerated, sycophancy à la Uriah Heap may be suspected!

The third measurement requires a little counting. Find words in the body of the writing that contain the same number of letters as in the word(s) of the signature, including a capital letter, e.g. 'However' and 'Simpson', and compare the horizontal length of the words.

A *longer* signature indicates that the writer is openly showing himself for all to view. A *shorter* signature indicates a writer who is holding a part of himself back from public gaze. The greater difference, the more emphasised is the interpretation. If the size difference is extreme, then the writer is either grossly flaunting or concealing himself.

Legibility of signature
If a person were required to make a speech ending with the identification of the speaker, i.e. himself, and his listeners noted a marked difference between the clarity of the speech content and the speaker's self-identification, a note of discord would be heard. Keeping this analogy in mind, consider the following possibilities...

Illegible writing with a legible signature
(A gabbled speech with a clear speaker identification at the end!) Eccentric to say the least! Such a writer is attaching more importance to conveying his own identity than to the content of his message. Emphasis upon self-importance is such that mental disturbance may be conjectured.

Illegible writing with an illegible signature
(A gabbled, inaudible speech followed by an equally gabbled, inaudible speaker identification.) Two possible reasons, the commonest being sheer impatience with having to write and the writer not really minding whether he is understood or not. The second, more unusual possibility is some impediment to successful communication, such as drugs or immense anxiety.

Legible writing with an illegible signature

(A clearly audible speech followed by a mumbled self-identification.) The writer is placing more emphasis upon communicating his thoughts than on revealing his identity — perhaps he is so sure of his status that he believes readers will instantly recognise who he is; alternatively, he may regard his own identity as largely insignificant compared with the content of his message and, as a result, may minimise the effort to communicate his name. Other measurements within the writing will point to the correct assessment.

Signature rendered partly or wholly illegible by the writer crossing it out

(The speaker who gives his name and then asks his audience to ignore it!) This has very negative interpretations — criticism of own ego, self-directed anger, self-destruction. If the whole signature has been affected, this feature may be one of the first signs of a suicidal tendency.

Illegible 'business' signature

The illegible scrawl that serves as a signature on many business letters is an indication that the writer saw no purpose in revealing his identity further than proving that 'someone' agreed the letter contents. This type of signature is most commonly found on letters where the writer is writing as a representative of the company or practice to which he belongs, rather than on his own personal behalf. The same writer is likely to sign with quite a different (and legible) signature when the letter in question is meant to convey his own personal and private opinions.

Placement of signature

Interpretation from the placement of a signature must be undertaken with due consideration made to the fact that business habits can impinge upon personal traits.

Left of page If not incorporated out of business habit, this is a sign of the writer's adherence to the past. Personal inhibition and possible feelings of disquiet towards the future are implied.

Middle of page The writer's placement of his public self in the centre of the 'stage' is a directive to his reader that he is to be the centre of their attention.

Right of page If extreme right, the writer is revealing an impulse to rush headlong into the future. If merely right of centre, the signature placement suggests the writer is moving forwards at an easy pace, neither anxious to leave the past behind nor to reach ahead of his capacities to make the future 'happen' all the sooner!

Additions to the signature

Underlining

Children are taught to ascribe importance to a word by underlining it. In the same way, an underlined signature has been awarded additional importance by the writer. This is a form of emphasis and is usually a sign that the writer feels a need to draw attention to his status.

Encircling

This is a gesture of self-protection and is indicative of the writer's desire to feel secure on all sides. As an extension to feeling 'sure', such a writer would be likely to check and double-check on possibilities — often as far as using tactics such as setting traps designed to identify possible opponents. This writer would be unlikely to leave anything to chance!

Elaboration
Elaborate additions to a signature illustrate the writer's desire to improve

his public image. Such elaboration is often seen in the capital letters where it can be interpreted as a desire for increased status and respect. If greatly exaggerated, the desire for an enhanced public image is equally magnified.

An additional conclusion may be drawn from the increased elaboration, size or pressure applied to just one, rather than all, capital letter. The fact that the writer feels a need to draw the reader's attention to one particular part of his signature is a clear indication of his affinity with that part of his name. If the emphasis is on a first name, it may be safely supposed that the writer is offering encouragement to his reader to know him by that name. If, however, the greater emphasis is on the initial letter of the last name, then the writer is obviously drawing attention to his surname — perhaps because it is a name carrying special status or, alternatively, because the writer is attempting to divert attention from his first name so as not to imply a desire to be known on first-name terms by the reader.

Full stop after signature
A signature at the end of a letter terminates that letter. A full stop, which means end, after the signature is somewhat superfluous in so much as the communication has already finished. The addition of the full stop serves to emphasise the fact that as far as the writer is concerned there is absolutely nothing more to be said. If a full stop follows a signature only occasionally, the writer is exhibiting a tendency to finish emphatically just on specific occasions, whereas when a full stop is an integral part of every signature the writer is revealing his liking for having the last word in every communication.

Angle
The angle of the signature signifies the 'push' or lack of it that the writer feels inclined to give his public image.

Signature and writing angle both the same

yours sincerely
Mr Jones

The writer is placing no undue emphasis upon the presentation of his public self: he is as he seems to be, indoors as well as out!

Signature left, writing right

yours sincerely

Miss Smith

The writer is pulling back on presentation of self. This is an unusual and often temporary reaction to a specific situation — somewhat akin to the swift withdrawal of burnt fingers.

Signature right, writing left or upright

yours sincerely

Mr Brown

The writer is presenting a more outgoing public image than he actually possesses. This may be a 'rising to the occasion' situation or perhaps a demonstration of the artificially outgoing public face some naturally introverted people manufacture for themselves.

Signature upright, writing left or upright

yours sincerely

Mr White

This writer lacks spontaneity, but has poise! He is able to control the degree of self-exposure even though he is not naturally very outgoing.

Direction

The rise or fall of a signature must be assessed along with the main body of writing. It is when the signature takes a different direction from that of the writing that special attention ought to be paid.

Rising

A sign of rising spirits, optimism, ambition and vitality.

Falling
A sign of falling spirits, pessimism, disappointment and lack of vitality.

The personal pronoun 'I'

The child who says 'I eat', 'I go' or 'I will' is demonstrating that he is the initiator of action. A less mature child refers to self as 'me' — 'me eat', 'me go' or 'me will'. The changeover from 'me' to 'I' puts into words the realisation that self is the subject, not the object, of the verb. 'I' is a reflection of each person's view of self; the personal pronoun 'I' represents the very core of the writer's personal image. During a single hour changes in how we view our inner selves can, and do, take place. Anyone who has ever experienced the feelings of despair and self-depreciation which accompany the wait for examination results to be pinned up, followed by that surge of sheer relief and self-confidence which follows the sight of one's name *above* rather than below the line, will know exactly what I mean. Writing samples taken just before and just after such an event would reveal the change in personal image as 'I' blossomed forth on the crest of the wave, albeit after a very shaky beginning.

There is a fascinating comparison to be made between an individual's private image of himself ('I') and the public image he presents to others (the signature).

Slant

Personal pronoun 'I' and signature both slanting in the same direction
There is no indication of conflict between this writer's public and private images.

'I' left, signature right The writer is inwardly unsure and cautious, but conceals these feelings by adopting an outgoing image.

'I' right, signature left This writer is both outgoing and self-assured, but feels uneasy: there is a possible conflict between the writing contents and her public image.

Size
'I' and signature of equal relative size There is little, if any, discrepancy between the writer's inner and outer confidence.

I , Miss Grey,

'I' smaller than signature The writer appears far more confident than she actually feels.

I , mr Wright

'I' larger than signature This writer has immense self-assurance which he is attempting to restrain.

I know

'I' out of proportion and exaggerated in size compared with the rest of the writing is associated with writers who are prone to fantasising.

i think, I know,

'I' written as a lower case 'i' or as a very small capital is indicative of a writer whose self-image is extremely low.

I Like

'I' written like a money sign indicates a writer whose thinking frequently revolves around money.

I think London

'I' tallest of all letters is a sign of self-esteem.

'I' tall with an inflated upper loop is an indication of a writer who has immense self-esteem but whose vanity may evaporate under pressure — there is a hint of wishful thinking here.

'I' tall with large, but narrow, upper loop is indicative of a writer with a need for a lofty status.

'I' containing excessive elaboration signifies a distinct lack of aesthetic taste.

| do this (of course!)

A straight 'I' made with a single stroke is a sign of the writer's appreciation of simplicity and straight-forwardness.

'I' swinging towards the left indicates the writer's leanings towards sentimentality.

I think

'I' with sharply angular formation is a sign of pugnacity.

I think

'I' with simple formation and begun with a 'tick' is the sign of a concise thinker.

I'll wait

'I' having a 'lassoo' formation indicates shrewdness and a favouring of tactics.

I know

'I' printed in otherwise cursive writing is a sign of constructive independence.

I cannot

'I' retraced is indicative of repression.

I always

'I' knotted is a sign of self-centredness.

2 am not

'I' shaped like the number 2 implies that the writer feels self to be second-class, physically or mentally, and has, as a result, learned to shield true reactions. Such writers often avoid relating intimately, thereby making them appear very independent.

'I' size or shape changing within one sample is an accurate pointer to the way an individual's private self image stands up to the passage of time. Where the size of the letter diminishes, the writer is unable to maintain his original stand, whereas an increase would show the writer's shaky start but gradual development of the courage of his own convictions.

Honesty or dishonesty?

Before we can even attempt to identify dishonest personality traits as they appear in writing, we must first be sure of what is meant by the word 'honesty'.

Honest people are 'good' people? Good people are diplomatic, kind and law abiding?...and yet...we know of good people who have, in the name of diplomacy, adjusted the truth to maintain the status quo. We know of good people who have, in the name of kindness, left honest comment unsaid. We know of good people who, in the name of the law, have punished the innocent and rewarded the guilty.

There is no simple method of defining honesty. It is the product of a combination of many factors and it would be a great mistake to point to any one action, whether written or otherwise, and take it as proof of the perpetrator's honesty or, indeed, of their guilt.

Each and every one of us has both a positive and a negative side to our nature. We all can, and all do, break rules. We all attempt to manipulate circumstances to our own benefit — in fact if we did not, we wouldn't be human.

We are all, therefore, dishonest. I believe it is only the degree of dishonesty that distinguishes the 'good' from the 'bad', the 'honest' from the 'dishonest'.

The 'honest' person tries to avoid deception and is straightforward in conduct; the writing of such a person ought to reflect the same clear qualities. Consistency of behaviour is mirrored in uniformity of style. The baseline upon which the middle zone rests should be reasonably level and the overall pressure should be firm and regular. If there is additional ornamentation, it ought not in any way interfere with legibility.

The 'dishonest' person has a predisposition to deceive others (and sometimes himself). There are many writing features which point towards possible dishonesty in the writer. They exist in everyone's writing to varying degrees; therefore, to determine a strong likelihood of dishonesty it is necessary to find at least seven of these features in a given sample of writing. After discovering the consistent presence of seven such signs, any additional features in the writing are indicative of the degree of dishonesty.

Examples

1. Two or more very different styles of writing — possibly more than one personality.

2. Signature very different from rest of writing — artificial outer persona.

3. Very large, over-embellished or highly ornamental writing — grandiose aspirations.

4. Over-complicated or over-simplified writing resulting in loss of legibility — deception.

5. Extremely light pressure — easily influenced.

6. Words with clear beginnings and endings but containing threaded middles — clear outer image concealing inner deviousness.

7. Illegible writing — unable or unwilling to make effort to communicate clearly.

8. Letters partially or totally omitted — parts of information omitted.

9. Broken letters — anxiety or uncertainty.

10. Unusual starting strokes — tendency to initiate action in an odd way.

11. Left-angled writing — unwilling to reveal inner views.

pie in the sky.

12. Very large or over-inflated upper zone — ambitions not always related to reality.

give

13. Very large or over-inflated lower zone — desires difficult to fulfil.

14. Sudden unrhythmical changes in pressure — sudden changes of mood intensity.

remain   aloof

and   independent

15. Very wide spaces between words and between lines — ability to remain detached or indifferent.

and then I am going to see Susie who I feel

16. Tangled spacing to detriment of legibility — actions are unnecessarily complicated.

17. Ornate or otherwise over complicated letter formations (such as coiling) — cunning tactician.

18. End strokes drawn to left in an emphasised, prolonged and deliberate way — resentment felt towards past, often stemming from negative experience during formative years.

19. Excessively high capital letters — great desire for status.

20. Excessively straight base line — calculation and concealment.

21. Very erratic baseline — adapts behaviour very easily and without forethought.

trace this and see what I mean by slow.

22. Very slow writing — lack of spontaneity, and hesitation.

and I will

23. Predominantly arcaded and angular with heavy pressure — aggression and resentment.

24. Combination of excessive ornamentation and inflated loops — high level of personal vanity.

25. Combination of dominant lower zone, hooked endings and coiling — acquisitiveness.

26. Combination of arcades, threads and closed, tight letter forms — secretiveness.

27. Combination of narrow upper margin, angular formations, counter strokes and uneven rhythm — anti-social.

28. Combination of erratic slant, spacing and rhythm plus strongly varied placement of 't' crossing, exaggerated loops and general irregular appearance — emotional instability.

29. Combination of strongly sinuous baseline, irregular letter sizes, threads plus varied placement of 't' crossings — weak will power.

30. Inflexibility or over-flexibility of slant, pressure, size and spacing — nervous tension or anxiety.

31. 't' crossings and 'i' dots to the left of the letter stem — caution.

write (write)
please (please)

32. Individual letters replaced by invented 'letter' forms — invented information replaces the truth.

33. *Any* gross exaggeration or over-simplification which interferes with the object of the exercise of writing, i.e. communication of ideas, is a negative sign and indicates a writer's inability, or purposeful lack of desire, to communicate openly and easily.

Doodles

Doodling is a way of marking time. A doodle is a conscious or unconscious written or drawn manifestation; it may or may not incorporate or embellish writing. It may take the form of a clearly recognisable picture, an intricate construction, or it may be little more than a virtually shapeless blob.

A doodle is often repetitious and most people have their own personal repertoire of doodles which they use over and over again. The one thing that doodles have in common is that they are all the result of the doodler having to wait before being able to make a desired action.

Think about what you are usually doing when you doodle. To save time I will give you the answer — wherever you are, if you are doodling you are waiting. If you are in the middle of a telephone conversation and you are doodling, you are waiting for something to happen, such as for the other person to stop talking and let you get a word in. Examine an 'on the telephone' doodle and with a little thought you will find that the doodle acts as a direct link with the doodler's subconscious urges.

A repetitious pattern, such as a flower, a heart or a star, drawn and re-drawn (each time a little more perfectly in my case) is an exercise begun and completed. The completed image apparently did not satisfy so the whole exercise was repeated and completed and repeated and completed until the doodler achieved his object of finishing satisfactorily. This repetition of completing an image is a clear signpost to the doodler's desire to terminate something. Such a doodle during a telephone call usually means that the doodler wants to finish the conversation. If for some reason the conversation suddenly picks up, the doodler's interest is awakened and far from wanting to finish he wants to keep the whole thing going. So what does he do with his doodle? He starts joining everything up and making it

into one ongoing design, and then he stops doodling and concentrates all his thought on the conversation.

The opposite is found in the doodler whose wish is to expand the conversation and who quietly beavers away at his doodle waiting for a pause in which to insert another question to extend the intercourse still further. His doodle will grow in size and incorporate all sorts of offshoots and interesting deviations, and then BINGO! He has got what he wanted, the conversation is finished and low and behold he has found a way to finishing the seemingly never ending amoeba-like growth of his doodle by putting it into a box (presumably to store it away for future reference).

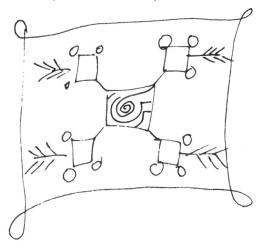

What of the doodler who embellishes? Embellishment can take more than one form: it may mean the addition of intricate detail, or it can cause the original doodle to grow in overall size.

The person who adds detail is revealing a desire to add depth to what he is doing/talking about. The doodler whose doodle gradually increases in size is looking to enlarge upon the subject. If the enlargement changes the context of the original doodle out of all recognition, the doodler's aim would appear to be to shift attention to the overall situation rather than to concentrate on one specific.

The doodler who is waiting to terminate an irritating conversation tends to make simple, complete angular doodles; while the friendly doodler who does not want to be rude, but who is nevertheless looking for a way out, will produce more rounded, but equally complete, doodles.

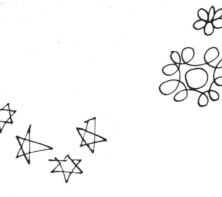

A point to keep in mind is that people do not doodle when they are concentrating on something else. Their doodling betrays their lack of concentration plus what they intend should happen next. Being forced to wait without the means to doodle does not act as a deterrent to poor concentration. On such an occasion doodling is done invisibly. People fidget, they twitch, they scratch, they write in dust, they pick at things, they embellish themselves (hair, nails, etc.) They rearrange things (other than themselves), such as telephone books or pocket contents. They wind their watches, they tap their feet. They do everything and anything rather than confine themselves to what they are actually engaged in, i.e. waiting. If on the telephone, they may indulge in silent conversations with companions and then when all patience has evaporated they often fib their way out of the conversation by describing a fictitious appointment/ visitor's arrival or, if desperate, they smell something burning.

Although it is sometimes said that a particular object in doodle form

carries its own interpretation whoever its originator, i.e. a heart doodle signifies that the doodler is a romantic, I find such an interpretation to be far too simplistic and, therefore, inaccurate. A heart drawn by a young impressionable female may indeed be an expression of her romanticism. But the same heart doodled by a butcher may carry rather gruesome connotations. An artist working on designs for next year's Valentine cards may doodle a heart with no thought whatsoever other than how to incorporate the darned thing into an original design, whereas the seller of those Valentine cards may regard the heart as symbolic of money in the bank.

Research has shown me that doodles fall into one of two categories, either the material and technical world (forms and structures), or the human and social world (relationships and appearances).

Forms and structures

Such doodles point to a writer's drive for achievement and an interest in the material and technical world. Such doodles consist of forms and structures of building and development.

Relationships and appearances

A mouth could represent kissing, speaking or eating, i.e. sex, communication, hunger. The sort of questions that arise are whether there is only one mouth and whether it is part of a face or complete by itself. Is it smiling, pouting or grimacing? The woman who doodles a glamourous face or figure may well be revealing hidden aspirations. A name written and re-written, often in slightly or greatly different forms, is a sign of a writer's desire to understand that person better − this is all the more interesting when the name is the writer's own: doodling one's own name is equivalent to doodling one's public face. Any elaborations incorporated in name mirror the outer persona improvements the writer wishes to 'try on for size'. A nice example of this is the doodle of the *new* name which saunters out of the pens of virtually all engaged-to-be-married women. The doodler is revealing a very great deal about her attitude to the role of wife as by trial and error she decides which part of the full name should be given emphasis.

When assessing a doodle, therefore, a two-fold interpretation may be made. The first conclusion to be reached is what it was the doodler was waiting for. The second, rather deeper, interpretation is a reflection of the doodler's own drives and ambitions.

There *are* non-doodlers but they are rare birds. Such people do not doodle because they refuse to mark time. If required to wait, they resist. Jim Ward, a nice Liverpudlian carpenter neighbour of mine, epitomises the non-doodler type. When required to wait, say for a delivery of timber, he enquires the length of the expected wait and sets off to do something else, returning at the appropriate time (like most non-doodlers he is a stickler for time). If the waiting time is inexact he gets someone else to do the waiting for him by telling them where he will be and to call him when the van comes. Non-doodlers do not wait for buses, neither do they indulge in small talk. Their communication tends to be straight to the point, their telephone bills are small and their telephone books remain unsullied, unless of course they share a telephone with a doodler!

The interpretation of changing writing trends

There is a fixed structure to handwriting that changes only gradually and over a long period of time. It is the fixed handwriting features that determine a writer's consistent personality profile.

Examination will, however, reveal aspects of writing which *do* change — usually in response to changes in the environment and circumstances which affect our daily lives.

By careful use of the ACORN chart, it is possible to monitor these more frequent changes in handwriting and to determine how well the writer is coping with the excitement or stress of daily life. (ACORN is a way of assessing personality traits from whether specific features are written **A**lways, **C**onsistently, **O**ccasionally, **R**arely or **N**ever.)

Regular measurements taken over a period of time will accurately chart the ebbs and flows of life forces. Due notice must be paid to emotional changes which are caused by the female menstrual cycle. Women wishing to monitor their own writing would be best to use a writing sample from about a week after the end of their period.

The ACORN chart is in two parts and I recommend that the examples on pages 122 and 130 be copied for your own use. To illustrate how best to use the ACORN chart two reproduced letters (identity of writers to be revealed later) are duly charted.

The measurement chart

See Chart 1 on the next page. To obtain accurate measurements of handwriting trends it is necessary to analyse large, rather than small, writing samples — preferably not much less than fifty words in a sample. The list on the left side of the chart is the one to be referred to in measurement taking.

I recommend that rather than write directly on the chart you use a piece

Chart 1

A C O R N

	A	C	O	R	N	
1 large lower zone						small lower zone
2 heavy pressure						light pressure
3 carefully formed						neglect
4 even alignment (baseline)						uneven alignment (baseline)
5 regular						irregular
6 slow						fast
7 small						large
8 small upper zone						large upper zone
9 small middle zone						large middle zone
10 left slant						right slant
11 space empty						space filled
12 narrow writing						wide writing
13 thin writing						thick writing
14 angles						garlands
15 linear						aesthetic
16 falling lines						rising lines
17 disconnected						connected
18 not rhythmical						rhythmical

A C O R N

of tracing paper and make your measurements on that. Not only does this ensure ease of transferring your findings to the second chart but also means that you will not use up chart copies at an alarming rate.

The measurements are easily achieved by careful examination of the writing sample. To clarify any misunderstanding as to what the analyst is looking for, here is a brief explanation of each feature.

1   Large lower zone
To achieve a place in the 'A' column the zone would have to be grossly exaggerated in size and/or emphasis. Placement in 'C' would indicate that this zone is consistently larger than the other two zones. An 'O' placement would indicate that there were occasions when the lower zone was the largest. 'R' would mean that these were few and far between. 'N' means small lower zone.

2   Heavy pressure
An 'A' column place would indicate extremely heavy pressure throughout.

'C' would be consistently heavy pressure but with some lessening of pressure on upward and leftward strokes. An 'O' place would indicate occasional incidents of heavy pressure. 'R' would mean that an increase of pressure could be seen but was not a part of the regular pattern of writing. 'N' means light pressure writing.

3 Carefully formed

An 'A' placement would indicate that the writer had paid both time and attention to the careful formation of letter forms. There would be no evidence of slovenly, simplified or neglected formation. A 'C' place would indicate that although the writing was formed carefully there were a *few* instances where speed or simplification had caused the writer to change some of the letter forms. An 'O' place would indicate the writer's desire to attain careful letter formations and also an overall desire to simplify letter forms. Attention may have been lavished on capitals and a number of other letters but simplification was of greater magnitude. 'R' would mean that care was exercised *very* infrequently. 'N' means neglected writing.

4 Even alignment

Attention is paid here to a combination of the regularity of the baseline itself and the evenness of alignment between baselines. An 'A' placement would indicate extremely straight baselines which were exactly aligned with each other. 'C' would mean the same as 'A' but with due allowance made for the fact that the writer is not a machine and, therefore, slight undulation is quite normal. 'O' would indicate the writer's attempt to achieve alignment in the face of a natural inclination for the pen to go elsewhere. 'R' is the same as above but with the writer's success rate being extremely low. 'N' means uneven alignment.

5 Regular

For 'regularity' read 'sameness'. An 'A' placement would indicate regularity verging upon monotony. 'C' would indicate regularity with occasional departures. 'O' would mean that the writer's attempts to maintain regularity were frequently superseded by more spirited manifestations. 'R' would reveal that the writer rarely managed to attain a semblance of sameness. 'N' means irregular writing.

6 Slow

Slow could mean pedantic or careful. Speed can be measured both by the eye and also by tracing over the writing. 'A' means excruciatingly slow. 'C' means consistently slow but with a few faster movements. 'O' indicates the existence of a fair number of slowly written formations. 'R' means very few slowly written formations and 'N' means fast writing.

7 Small

Measure writing from the top of the upper zone to the bottom of the lower zone (Copybook is usually 9mm). 'A' is all writing less than 9mm. 'C' is writing which is consistently, but not totally, smaller than 9mm. 'O' is writing that contains occasional 'dips' below 9mm. 'R' is the very rare appearance of such 'dips'. 'N' means large writing.

8 Small upper zone

Compare the size of the upper zone with the other two zones. 'A' would mean the upper zone is always the smallest. 'C' would mean that although the upper zone was consistently small there were a few occasions when it poked up a bit sufficiently to equal one of the other zones. 'O' would mean that the upper zone was occasionally smaller than the other two. 'R' would mean that on very few occasions the upper zone was smaller than the other two zones. 'N' means large upper zone.

9 Small middle zone

Everything written about the upper zone applies here with the necessary exchange of the word 'middle' for the word 'upper'.

10 Left slant

'A' means always. 'C' means consistent but with a few departures. 'O' points to an occasional sally to the left. 'R' indicates that the left sallies are very rare happenings. 'N' means upright or right-slanted writing.

11 Space empty

The space in question is that between letters, words and lines. An 'A' placement indicates wide gulfs between all. 'C' is a sign of lots of empty space with a few departures from that norm. 'O' means that the writer leaves the occasional big space. 'R' means these spaces require looking for. 'N' means space filled.

12 Narrow writing

To establish narrowness either ascertain it by eye alone or, to be quite sure, draw a little box around a large selection of middle zone letters. Copybook writing would result in a square box. Wide writing would result in a wide oblong. Narrow writing would result in a tall oblong. A similar box drawn around capital letters in Copybook writing would equal two perfect squares, one on top of the other. Wide writing capitals would produce a tall oblong comprising of less than two squares one on top of the other. Narrow writing capitals would result in a tall oblong shape into which more than just two perfect squares could be piled. An 'A' placement would mean that all the writing is narrow. A 'C' placement would indicate that although the writing was consistently narrow there were a few occasions where it was not. An 'O' place would be the best choice when the letter width varied between narrow and Copybook. An 'R' placement would indicate the inclusion of a few narrow letters in an otherwise medium or wide script. 'N' means wide writing.

13 Thin writing

Curiously thin writing, like its opposite number, thick or pasty writing, is often judged to be easy to recognise but very difficult to describe.

Imagine you are watching two ice skaters. There will be one whose skates stay virtually the same distance apart, no matter how they turn and whirl. All the movement is in the skater's body — the motion is often slow and sensuous. Enter the other sort of skater, body rigid and feet twirling and twisting. This skater's progress is far more erratic and certainly lacking in the almost languid movement of his colleague.

Thin writing contains all that clever 'footwork'. The writer's fingers and pen do a lot of work. The thick or pasty writer is more relaxed; the pen and fingers move more smoothly and with a rounded grace. These writers often favour a thick-nibbed pen. If you feel unsure about judging this feature by eye alone, take up that empty ballpoint pen and follow the writer's (skater's) movements for yourself. Thin writing has corners and intricate parts; thick writing corners smoothly and avoids retracing. Imagine some writing made of wire, with the same word created twice — one form thick and and the other thin. If the two pieces of wire were pulled straight and compared, the one which comprised the thin word would be the longest.

An 'A' indicates corners, details and retracing throughout the writing. 'C' indicates much fancy footwork with the occasional gentle swirl. 'O' has numerous swirls but also has some corners and intricacies. 'R' undulates with a few rarely encountered corners cropping up. 'N' means thick writing.

14 Angles

Look for the angles in both connections and letter forms. An 'A' means that the writing has angles all over the place, both between and within the letters. A 'C' placement indicates an overall angularity with a few rounded shapes. 'O' means a mixture of both garland and angle. 'R' means mostly rounded with the occasional angle. 'N' means garlanded writing.

15 Linear

A linear writer is one who chooses to concentrate upon getting the facts across and the writing properly done rather than spending time and effort upon adding or subtracting parts of the writing to make it aesthetically more pleasing or original. Layout will be straightforward rather than eyecatchingly balanced. The writing style will be close to Copybook. 'A' would be writing which was totally lacking in elaboration or a sense of display. 'C' would also exclude much elaboration but would have the occasional spark of originality. 'O' would be neither wildly individualistic nor starkly practical. 'R' would have changed quite a lot from Copybook but would still retain a few of its features. 'N' means that the writer has employed his artistic licence throughout both layout and letter formation.

16 Falling lines

As writing should progress on the horizontal from left to right, falling lines are easy things to see. 'A' means the writing looks as though, given very little encouragement, it will shortly slip off the page. 'C' means it is on the way down but it does manage to even up in places. 'O' indicates overall straight writing which contains some downward tendencies. 'R' indicates horizontal lines. 'N' means rising lines.

17 Disconnected

Copybook words consist of letters joined together. 'A' indicates there are no connections. 'C' means that the writing is mostly disconnected but contains some connections. 'O' is writing with half its letters connected and the other half disconnected. 'R' means that the writing is mostly connected with a few breaks. 'N' means connected writing.

18 Not rhythmical

Rhythmical writing, like rhythmical speech, moves harmoniously along. Writing which lacks rhythm often has slants to both the left and the right, large and small middle zone letters, differing formations and a generally haphazard appearance. 'A' indicates an overall disjointed, unrhythmical appearance. 'C' is consistently unrhythmical but has some regularities. 'O' has some displeasing or haphazard formations. 'R' is rhythmical but careful observation will note a few irregularities. 'N' means rhythmical writing.

Dear Mr Simpson.

Thank you for your letter dated 16th June - you of course I would be delighted to grant you permission to use my hand writing - I hope the above is ok. - with best wishes yours sincerely

This sample of writing has been reproduced at ninety per cent of its original size.

And now a look at a real sample of writing (see the previous page). The writer is male and is in his thirties...

1   Large lower zone?

This means large as compared with the other two zones. Comparison must be made throughout the sample. Although the word 'grant' has a very large lower zone the 'delighted' has an upper and lower zone of about the same size. Overall examination will reveal that the lower zone is the largest zone on occasion rather than rarely or consistently. Therefore the 'O' column is duly filled in.

2   Heavy pressure?

Examination reveals firmer pressure on down strokes than on up strokes. Words 'would' and 'above' contain letters ('d' and 'b' respectively) in which the writer has chosen to lift his pen right off the page during the up stroke. The pressure is not heavy overall but does contain some firmness. Again my choice is the 'O' column.

3   Carefully formed?

Although this writing is certainly not pretty, there are no letter points which have been omitted and thus interfere with legibility. Neither care nor neglect are strongly apparent. 'O' column again!

4   Even alignment (of the base line)?

Although not rigidly formed, the base lines are reasonably straight and contain only natural undulation. 'C' column.

5   Regular?

Yes! The writing, although perhaps a little unorthodox, is formed with regularity; the same shapes and angles are used throughout the letter. 'C' column.

6   Slow?

An empty ball point pen or stylus run over this writing reveals an interesting anomaly. Although each letter is written quickly, the writer has disconnected virtually every letter, thus slowing down his writing dramatically. 'C' column.

7   Small?

This is with reference to the overall size — tip of upper zone to tip of lower zone. Definitely larger than the prescribed 9mm. Column 'N'.

8 Small upper zone?
No; although the upper zone is occasionally overshadowed by the writer's lower zone, it usually reigns supreme. This is especially the case with his capital letters, with the one exception of the personal pronoun 'I' and we all know what that means don't we? (You jolly well ought to if you have read the book through!!) 'R' column.

9 Small middle zone?
The smallest zone of the three but with a tendency to 'rise to the occasion' at the beginning of words: see 'permission' and 'with'. Column 'C'.

10 Left slant?
No. But occasional little falters make themselves apparent: see the 't' in the words 'dated' and 'best'. Column 'O'.

11 Space empty?
A mixture here. The writing is spread out to give an overall impression of fullness. There are, however, wide spaces between words and lines. Column 'C'.

12 Narrow writing?
No. Letters are mostly wide and the breaks between the letters make the words wider still. Occasional narrow letters, such as the letter 'r' in the word 'permission', mean that column 'N' is ruled out. Column 'R'.

13 Thin writing?
A mixture. Column 'O'.

14 Angles?
There is difficulty in finding any connections to measure and there are few angles within the letters themselves. Column 'R'.

15 Linear?
There are no additional elaborations in the writing, neither does the spacing indicate a penchant for an interest in layout. Column 'C'.

16 Falling lines?
No. The lines of writing are either horizontal or rising. Column 'N'.

Chart 2

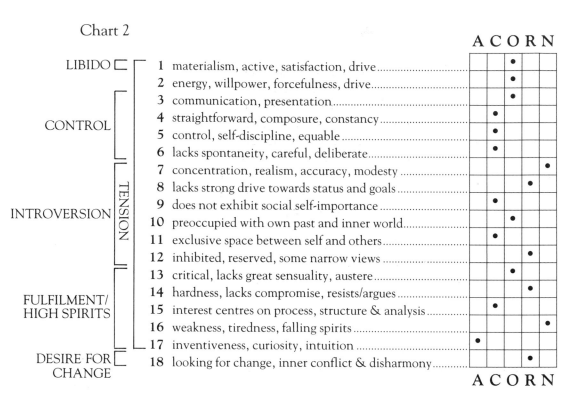

Category	#	Trend	A	C	O	R	N
LIBIDO	1	materialism, active, satisfaction, drive			•		
	2	energy, willpower, forcefulness, drive			•		
CONTROL	3	communication, presentation			•		
	4	straightforward, composure, constancy		•			
	5	control, self-discipline, equable		•			
	6	lacks spontaneity, careful, deliberate		•			
INTROVERSION (TENSION)	7	concentration, realism, accuracy, modesty					•
	8	lacks strong drive towards status and goals				•	
	9	does not exhibit social self-importance		•			
	10	preoccupied with own past and inner world			•		
	11	exclusive space between self and others		•			
	12	inhibited, reserved, some narrow views				•	
FULFILMENT/ HIGH SPIRITS	13	critical, lacks great sensuality, austere			•		
	14	hardness, lacks compromise, resists/argues				•	
	15	interest centres on process, structure & analysis		•			
	16	weakness, tiredness, falling spirits					•
DESIRE FOR CHANGE	17	inventiveness, curiosity, intuition	•				
	18	looking for change, inner conflict & disharmony			•		

A C O R N

17 Disconnected?
A resounding yes! The connections are so very few and far between that they may be discounted. Column 'A'.

18 Not rhythmical?
Apart from one or two pull-backs, the writing does have a somewhat loose limbed but definite rhythm to it. Column 'R'.

If in doubt between two measurements, award half a point to each. Now place the tracing paper over Chart 2.

.... lack of materialism, repressed appetites   1

...................................limited energy, willpower or forcefulness   2

.... leaves unfinished, neglects standards   3

.... lack of constancy of direction, erractic   4

.... lack of control, mood changes, unpredictable   5

.... impulsive, spontaneous, liveliness   6

.... exaggeration, ambition, enjoys/seeks attention   7

.....................goal- and status-orientated, high aspirations   8

....exhibits social self-importance   9

.... demonstrative, outgoing, future-orientated   10

.... needs and wants close involvement with others   11

.....................lacks inhibition, expansive horizons, obtrusive   12

.....................sensuality, warmth, personal luxury, tactile   13

.... receptive, yielding, kind, natural   14

...visually minded, interested in shape, colour & appearance   15

.... rising spirits, humour, ambition, vitality   16

.... logic, will finish what was begun, singlemindedness   17

.... at one with self, content, adapts smoothly to change   18

Add columns A, C, O, R, N.
Add together the totals in A & C, and R & N...thus making THREE numbers,

$$\text{e.g.} \quad \begin{matrix} \text{A C O R N} \\ 2\ 4\ 5\ 3\ 3 \end{matrix} = \begin{matrix} \text{A+C, O, R+N} \\ 6 \quad 5 \quad 6 \end{matrix} = 6/5/6$$

To assess tension and release add columns 1 to 17 (inclusive)
To assess control and lack of control add columns 3 to 6 (inclusive)
To assess introversion or extroversion add columns 7 to 12 (inclusive)
To assess fulfilment add columns 13 to 17 (inclusive)
To assess strong or repressed libido consider column 1
To assess dissatisfaction or satisfaction with the present situation consider
  column 18

Re Tension and Release An ideal score would be a balanced number, with
the first and third numbers being equal. A high score on A+C and a low
score on R+N indicate that the writer needs to find a release from a build-

up of tension. Analysis of the A+C column will reveal where the tension is coming from. A low score on A+C and a high score on R+N indicate a writer who is allowing the situation to run away with him; such a writer needs to take careful stock of the direction he is taking. Analysis of the R+N columns will reveal those areas most in need of 'pruning'.

A high score in column O and comparatively low scores in A+C and R+N indicate a more temperate personality – the sort of person who manages to amble along through life without registering exaggeratedly high or low reactions.

When the ACORN chart is used regularly any changes of rhythm will be accurately charted. There are some people who, because of the demands of their jobs or their natural inclinations, regularly build up monumental highs of tension which are followed by monumental releases. People who work to demanding deadlines are good examples of this tendency towards extreme highs and lows. It is, therefore, important to take measurements over a period of time and compare results...the seemingly maniacal tendencies of actors and actresses often being a perfectly natural and *most necessary* release of the tension built up before the show...'IF YOU SEE WHAT I MEAN D-A-H-L-I-N-G!!!'

Re Control and Lack of Control A consistently high score of either A+C or R+N totals should be viewed negatively. Too much control is just as potentially harmful as lack of control. If there are extremes, their sources will be revealed by analysis of the more extreme traits. The writer should be able to glean valuable clues as to just where his 'grip' needs to be tightened (or loosened!)

Re Introversion or Extroversion Maintained extremes are never to the good. It is interesting to examine these measurements to find the way out for the introvert's shyness and the reason for the extrovert's drive. A writer who appears to be introverted overall is likely to find that examination of any features that pull to the right will reveal motivations which will bring him out of his shell. If, for instance, an introvert's most rightward tendency is towards goals and status, it is most likely that the desire to reach goals and gain recognition will provide the sort of motivation necessary for him to move towards more outgoing behaviour.

Re Fulfilment/High Spirits...love of life. High score in A+C would be indicative of the individual who is not inclined towards play. We *all* have such moments 'Don't be so SILLY!'), especially when we need to concentrate upon the job in hand. A consistently high score in this area is a little sad in a way; the writer would do well to examine his most rightward tendency, e.g. visually minded, etc. This would indicate the area he is most likely to be able to indulge himself in...interior design? painting lessons? Fulfilment/High Spirits is rarely overdone for any meaningful length of time — it tends to mellow after a while (as my old mother used to say, 'Let them enjoy themselves while they can...')

Re Libido Just like walking, we all move at the pace that suits us best. We can slow down or speed up according to the motivation at the time. This measurement is usually pretty consistent, but will reflect the ebbs and flows of individual passion!

Re Dissatisfaction or Satisfaction with the Present Situation Quite straightforward this one; consistently high A+C score indicates that the writer is not content to stay as he is and is actively seeking change. A consistently high R+N score smacks of complacency...tsk!

The interpretation chart
Taking the features one by one a general picture begins to emerge.
1 The writer has no great acquisitive drive nor does he reject possessions. His appetites are 'normal'.
2 His personal drives of energy, will-power and forcefulness are neither subdued nor exaggerated.
3 The attention he pays to presentation is reasonable. He neither neglects standards nor makes great play of the manner of presentation. He communicates in a positive way and neither embroiders nor neglects to give information.
4 There is a sense of control about his behaviour. He exercises self-discipline to achieve a level of predictability and sameness.
5 He is able to control his natural spontaneity by adopting a careful, rather deliberate, approach.
6 He enjoys taking centre stage especially when it is a means to achieving ambition. There is a move away from realism towards exaggeration, which implies his own awareness of the need to adopt a role on such occasions.
7 He is both goal- and status-minded. His aspirations are high.
8 His natural inclination does not lead him to exhibit social self-importance. His self-confidence is not as strong as it might be. (This may well account for the role he feels necessary to adopt as detailed in 6.)

9 His attitude to the past and future is balanced. He takes both into account when making decisions and planning.

10 He feels a need to maintain an exclusive space between himself and most other people. He tends to resist becoming closely involved. (A private person?)

11 He is not inhibited, particularly as he views his distant horizons. It is in an effort to reach these horizons that he will control his inner reserve and impress his views and himself on others.

12 He strikes a balance between personal indulgence and austerity. Although he can be both warm and sensual, his inner balance is such that when the occasion demands he is able to quell such feelings and adopt an impersonal attitude.

13 He has a natural and receptive manner and is prepared to yield to another rather than to refuse to consider compromise.

14 He is not artistically inclined. His interests centre on process and structure. He wants to know how a thing will be achieved rather than how it will look when it is finished.

15 At the time of writing, his spirits were rising (I suspect a smile as he wrote!)

16 When he sees a wood, he sees a group of trees. He is inventive, versatile and adaptive in preference to employing single-minded logic to what he encounters.

17 He is at one with his inner self and is preparing himself to adapt to what the future may bring.

These seventeen points combine to create an interesting, but rather disjointed, personality profile. It is possible, however, to combine certain of the measurements to obtain a fair indication of general trends.

Introversion/extroversion 2/1/3 is revealed by the combination of numbers 7 to 12. This writer is outgoing but is far from being a wholehearted extrovert. The three points that appear to pull him towards being outgoing (numbers 7, 8 and 12) have a common link with the future, ambition and goals. This implies that his extroversion is directed at the attaining of goals rather than at 'spreading himself around'. The two pulls away from extroversion (numbers 9 and 11) bond together natural modesty and a desire to keep himself to himself.

Control or lack of control 3/1/0 is revealed by combining features 3 to 6. The writer definitely has control of his affairs. His only lack in this direction seems to be a lack of finish or neglect of standards. The combination of the remaining three indicates a wealth of constancy, care and overall control; therefore, there is a strong likelihood that the pull towards lack of finish may be associated with outside influences such as environment and lack of time — both of which could account for a lack of 'polishing'. On no occasion will he willingly relinquish control.

Fulfilment/High Spirits 2/1/3 is revealed by combining features 13 to 17. Here there are two to the left and four to the right, so the writer *does* enjoy life. The only curtailments are a combination of 15 to 17, both of which appear linked to his endeavours and desire to understand processes and structures — aspects of work perhaps?

Libido 0/1/0 A middle-of-the-road tendency is revealed by feature 1. The writer is giving nothing away!

Tension and release 7/5/6 is revealed by combining numbers 1 to 17. Too much tension and we end up with an ulcer or worse. Too much release and euphoria rules to the exclusion of reality.

This writer's score reveals a slight leaning towards tension. Tension must always find a release: work hard, play hard. Sometimes sleep provides the deep, restful answer, but when the 'wind up' is too tight a 'wind down' *must* be found. His tension level is not alarming but a score of 6/6/6 would be better. (I hope his reading this interpretation provides release rather than a further increase of tension.)

So who is this slightly diffident, goal-orientated person who allowed me to use his writing as a sacrificial offering on my ACORN alter? None other than His Grace, The Duke of Westminster! My second example (see overleaf) contains a clue to the identity within the sample itself so rather than encourage you to turn immediately to the end of this chapter to confirm the writer's identity I have not bothered to remove his signature. Indeed, prior knowledge of this writer's identity may well make the ACORN findings all the more fascinating as they reveal themselves. First:

The measurement chart:

1 Large lower zone? The writer's lower zone is strong and even when it is small in actual size as in the word 'successful' it compares favourably with the other two zones which are also smaller. Column 'C'.

2 Heavy pressure? The pressure is reasonably, but not excessively, strong. The down and horizontal strokes contain especial firmness. Column 'C'.

3 Carefully formed? Not really; the writing is legible but this is achieved more by the overall sense of the sentence than by careful formation. Column 'R'.

Dear Diane.

I have no objection to your using my letter as part of the illustration in your new book.

Provided of course that you do not refer to me as "King Arthur".

Best wishes for a successful book

Yours

Arthur Scargill

"The Yorkshire Moderate"

This sample of writing has been reproduced at ninety per cent of its original size.

4 Even alignment? Although all the lines rise they do tend to vary both in angle of rise and in individual undulation. Column 'R'.

5 Regular? There is an overall sameness about this writing but it cannot be deemed to be regular because of the high number of inconsistencies. Column 'R'.

6 Slow? No! Apart from certain additional inflated formations in the capital letters, this writing was written at speed. Column 'R'.

7 Small? Size is rather variable. Most of the writing is on the large side but there are a few letters which do not exceed the Copybook size. Column 'R'.

8 Small upper zone? The upper zone is second in size to the lower and largest zone. Some of its formations are exaggerated as in the capital 'D's and 'P's and personal pronoun 'I'. Column 'R'.

9 Small middle zone? Although the smallest of the three zones, this writer's middle zone does not really lack size. It is variable though, see the word 'in' and the letters 'es' in the word 'successful'. Column 'R'.

10 Left slant? No! Column 'N'.

11 Space empty? There are wide spaces both between words and between lines. Column 'C'.

12 Narrow writing? Variable. Some letters are narrow, as demonstrated by the letter 'e' in the word 'the' and letter 'g' in the word 'using'. Whereas some letters have quite wide construction, such as the letter 'u' in the word 'you' and the letter 'a' in the word 'as'. Column 'O'.

13 Thin writing? Yes! Column 'C'.

14 Angles? This writing contains a wide mixture of connecting strokes — mostly threads — but there are some angles present. Column 'O'.

15 Linear? Yes! Column 'C'.

16 Falling lines? No! Column 'N'.

17 Disconnected? More connections than disconnections, but they are there. Column 'O'.

18 Not rhythmical? Yes! Column 'C'.

Interpretation

1 This writer has an active drive towards satisfying his appetites.
2 He is energetic, forceful and has a strong will.
3 His presentation tends to lack finish and, as a result, his communication may suffer.
4 There is a certain irregularity in his composure. His attitude may not always be straightforward.
5 He may be unpredictable and his control may slip on occasion.
6 A lively personality, he is spontaneous in his reactions but he should guard against impulsiveness.
7 He quite enjoys taking centre stage, especially when this is a means to achieving ambition. There is a move away from realism towards exaggeration, which implies his own awareness of his need to adopt a role on such occasions.
8 He is both goal- and status-minded. His aspirations are high.
9 He is self-confident and has a sense of self-importance.
10 He is demonstrative, outgoing and future orientated. He lacks any tendency to look to the past; he wishes to progress.
11 He feels a need to maintain an exclusive space between himself and most other people. He tends to resist becoming closely involved. (A private person?)
12 He is neither excessively obtrusive nor inhibited, but adapts his behaviour to the situation in which he finds himself.
13 His critical faculties are well honed and there is sometimes a rigidity and and an austerity in his manner.
14 His is not an 'affected' personality; he is receptive to ideas, but resists compromise. His behaviour is neither wholly hard nor wholly yielding.
15 He is not artistically inclined. His interests centre on process and structure. He wants to know how a thing will be achieved rather than how it will look when it is finished.
16 At the time of writing, his spirits were rising (I suspect a smile as he wrote!)
17 The writer is able to employ both logic and intuition. He is able both to follow through an action to its end *or* to separate ideas into different projects and depart from a seemingly set path to attain what he wants.

18 At the time of writing, the writer was not really happy with himself. There are signs of an inner conflict and a penchant for change.

General trends

Introversion/extroversion 1/1/6 This is an extrovert. The only aspect of self that pulls away from extroversion is his need to distance himself from other people.

Control or lack of control 0/0/4 His control is not good. His drive for achievement is extremely strong.

Fulfilment/Happiness 2/2/2 Neither ecstatic nor despondent. He may view life with a mixture of feelings.

Libido 1/0/0 There is nothing wrong here!

Tension and release 5/3/10 This degree of release could be dangerous — a little reminiscent of descending a steep hill on a bicycle with no brakes.

The pull-backs (1, 2, 11, 13, 15) from the brink appear to have a common theme relating to his inner qualities which include the satisfaction of own appetites, willpower, exclusion of self from others, firmness of control, criticism and interest in construction. It would appear that this man's 'brakes' can only be applied from within!

An especially interesting feature of this writing is the elaborate signature. But I felt rather startled by the end stroke that decapitates the surname (see signatures, page 102).

Summary

The ACORN chart will...quickly and easily...
○ help you identify causes of tension and indicate how best to deal with them (ulcer avoidance!)
○ help to show how to beat shyness
○ help you get more enjoyment out of life
○ help you become aware of your faults and indicate how best to combat them
○ give you a chart of personality strengths and weaknesses
○ identify the sources of problems and their solutions
○ draw attention to the onset of problems *before* they become a problem
○ enable you to know yourself as you really are, not the way you *think* you are

Handwriting analysis checklist

Copy this page and do *not* proceed to the next number until you have ticked the previous box. This applies to *every* analysis you undertake.

☐   1   Name or reference number of subject.

☐   2   Age of subject at time of writing.

☐   3   Sex of subject.

☐   4   Date sample was written.

☐   5   Date writing analysed.

☐   6   Object of analysis (general personality profile, recruitment, other(?))

☐   7   *First impressions:* write down everything that occurs to you, *no matter how seemingly illogical;* include overall look, personal reactions plus any obvious extremes or unusual features.

☐   8   ACORN chart (measurements only − *not* interpretation at this stage).

Carefully note your observations pertaining to all of the following:

☐ 9 Form level.

☐ 10 Size.

☐ 11 Speed.

☐ 12 Zones.

☐ 13 Baseline.

☐ 14 Slant.

☐ 15 Pressure.

☐ 16 Spacing.

☐ 17 Connections and letter shapes.

☐ 18 Beginnings and endings.

☐ 19 Specific letter formations.

☐ 20 Signature and personal pronoun 'I'.

☐ 21 Honesty/dishonesty.

☐ (22 Doodles.)

☐ 23 ACORN chart, measurements and interpretation.

Take the measurements all over again *without* referring to the first measurement you have taken on the ACORN chart. (Comparison of both charts will serve as a constant reminder of the need for accurate observation.) Use the *second* measurements as a basis for your interpretation.

You will now have a list of comprehensive statements and facts relating to the writer's personality. The more practice you have at assessment, the more smoothly the analyses will flow. Never forget that your role is that of an opinion-giver, not a judge. Conclusions, therefore, must be tempered with sensitive commonsense rather than with the critic's flaming sword. Anyway, didn't someone once say 'Judge not that ye be not judged'?!

Index